USBORNE

TRUE STORIES OF
EVEREST
ADVENTURES

This edition first published in 2015 by Usborne Publishing Ltd,
Usborne House, 83-85 Saffron Hill,
London EC1N 8RT, England.
www.usborne.com

A catalogue record for this title is available
from the British Library.

Printed in Hong Kong

Series editors: Jane Chisholm, Jenny Tyler and Rosie Dickins
Designer: Glen Bird
Series designer: Mary Cartwright
Illustrators: Glen Bird and John Woodcock
Cover designer: Amy Manning
Cover image © Look and Learn / Bridgeman Images

With grateful thanks to Audrey Salkeld for reading and commenting
on the manuscript; Kate and Keith Lee, The Old Bookshop,
Wolverhampton, for generously providing several rare and unusual
books; and Margaret Ecclestone of the Alpine Club Library.

PB ISBN: 9780794536510
ALB ISBN: 9781601304025

USBORNE

TRUE STORIES OF
EVEREST
ADVENTURES

PAUL DOWSWELL

CONTENTS

Into the death zone

Everest, the highest mountain in the world, towers 8,850m (29,035ft) above sea level – that's over 20 times taller than a skyscraper. Half in China, half in Nepal, it forms part of the Himalayas, a colossal mountain range stretching between India and China.

This map shows the location of Everest.

Many climbers have attempted to reach the top of Everest, but this is a goal fraught with peril. Everest climbers have to face treacherous mountain slopes, extreme weather and avalanches, only to reach altitudes which are dangerous in themselves. Climbers refer to heights above 5,800m (19,000ft) as "the death zone". Human beings were never designed to live at such an altitude, where there is only one third the usual amount of oxygen in the air. Yet despite these dangers, Everest has been climbed by at least 15 different routes.

The route that originally led mountaineers two-thirds of the way through the Earth's atmosphere, and onto the roof of the world, leads up the South East Ridge. This was the route taken by the first men to reach the summit, Edmund Hillary and Tenzing Norgay, in 1953. In the years since, over a thousand climbers have stood puffing and panting on top of the world's tallest mountain, on a summit said to be little bigger than a billiard table. This seems like a lot of people until you realize that over 170 climbers have died on Everest. For every four or so climbers who got to the summit, someone died on the mountain – frightening odds that still make getting to the top an extraordinary achievement.

Because the South East Ridge is by far the most popular route, the world's elite climbers tend to be a bit snooty about it. They refer to it dismissively as "The Yak Route", after the famously hairy cattle found in Tibet. But such talk is mountaineer bravado.

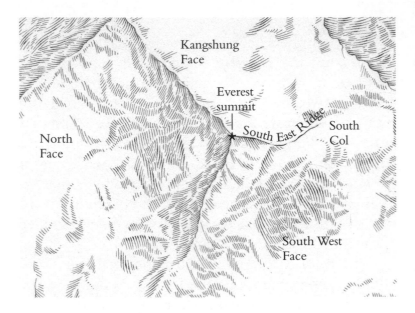

This aerial view of Everest shows all the faces of the mountain at once.

Any route up Everest is an endurance test and life gamble unimaginable to most ordinary people.

Even on the way up to the South East Ridge, a climber has to pass through a fractured glacier of tottering, cathedral-size blocks of ice, that could come crashing down on them without warning. Then they must reach a flat, dreary plain, around the size of a large sports stadium, called the South Col, which huddles between the twin peaks of Everest and its smaller companion Lhotse.

The South Col has been called the most desolate campsite in the world. Here, at 7,860m (26,200ft), the wind howls so constantly and loudly it is often likened to a jumbo jet at takeoff. The wind brings blizzards, and temperatures can drop as low as -40°C (-40°F). At this altitude, even the healthiest climber can feel as if they are suffering from a ferocious hangover. The body almost immediately begins to deteriorate – the lungs become clogged with mucus, the brain swells, eating and drinking become impossibly weary chores, and climbers become light-headed and easily confused. Because of this, most climbers on the mountain carry oxygen. The extra energy oxygen provides makes up for the additional weight of the breathing equipment. But even with this artificial aid, reaching the summit is still the most taxing, exhausting journey imaginable.

❖

Bodies on Everest are a frequent sight – especially this high up. Although some are brought down the mountain for burial, this can be an extremely dangerous procedure, so most are left where they died. After all, why risk another life for someone who is dead already? During the 1990s, one of the most pitiable sights on the South Col was the body of an Indian climber from an expedition in 1985. He could be seen crouched on his knees, leaning forward as if to open the zipper flap entrance on his tent, his face set in a grimace of utter misery.

Returning from a summit attempt, he had reached the safety of his tent only to find his frozen hands lacked the strength and dexterity to unzip the entrance. Perhaps he was too tired to call for help, but if he had done, his cries would have been carried away by the wind. Besides, his colleagues might well have been too weak to come to his aid – a climb up the South East Ridge can leave even the most experienced mountaineer so exhausted they can hardly speak. So, with his warm sleeping bag and the prospect of a stove and a hot drink a mere zip away, the climber died. In time, the fierce winds blew his tent to tatters, but his body remained, like a strange, frozen statue, reaching out to a safe spot that would be forever beyond his grasp.

❖

The final route to the top, up the knife edge of snow, ice and rock that make up the South East Ridge, is a seven or eight hour slog, or more. Climbers usually set off before daybreak, or even the night before, to ensure they reach the top in good time to return in daylight.

Getting to the top is only half the battle – on the way back, darkness and exhaustion can be a lethal combination, making coming down even more dangerous than going up. One wrong step can send a climber tumbling down the rock and scree of the South West Face, or plunging down the icy Eastern "Kangshung" Face – both falls of thousands of feet. One Everest expedition leader once remarked: "With enough determination, any b***** idiot can get up this hill – the trick is to get down alive."

The distance from the South Col to the summit is little more than a mile (1.6km). But it is also 1,200m (4,000ft) upwards, and by the time climbers are halfway there, they probably need to stop every two or three steps to get their breath back. Some determined climbers even drag themselves to the top on all fours. On Everest, even the best and most experienced climbers will take foolhardy risks to stand among the tattered flags, keepsakes and discarded equipment that now litter the summit.

If they succeed in reaching the summit and the weather is good, the view is astounding. Depending on the time of day, the shadow of Everest can stretch hundreds of miles over the dusty, brown plateau of Tibet, or it can hang magically in the atmosphere. Even the curvature of the Earth can be seen, along with Himalayan peaks over 160km (100 miles) away. Above, the sky is virtually black, and a climber can feel as if he or she is on the very edge of space.

Read on, and discover why it took 30 years of intense effort just to climb to the top of this forbidding peak, and marvel at the extraordinary adventures of the men and women who are driven by bravery, tenaciousness, determination and folly to stand on top of the world.

First steps to the Third Pole

The expedition of 1921

One cheerless January morning in 1921, British newspaper readers were treated to exciting news about the tallest mountain in the world. Typical of the reports was this, from *The London Daily Mail*:

> The decision to attempt the climbing of Mount Everest – the last and perhaps hardest of the great adventures to be achieved by man in the terrestrial world – was taken by the Royal Geographical Society at its meeting in London last night. The North and South Poles have both been conquered in this generation, but Everest, the mightiest mountain in the world, and a name of magic to all, still lifts its snowy peak unscaled to a level, according to the latest survey, of 29,140ft [8,740m], in the romantic recesses of the Himalayas between Nepal and Tibet.

As they read on, the public was left in no doubt as to the danger and difficulty of such an enterprise.

TOP OF THE WORLD – WILL HUMAN BODY STAND THE PRESSURE?

screamed a headline in *The Glasgow Citizen*. Only in

the previous two years had advances in aircraft design seen planes flying to heights as great as Everest. There was much interest in the practicalities of survival at such a high altitude. As *The Glasgow Citizen* reminded its readers: "At such heights it is very difficult to work. There is less oxygen in the air... the chief effect of the rarefied air is a feeling of lassitude [fatigue]."

It was exciting stuff. In the years before the First World War of 1914-18, the newspapers had been full of stories of Polar exploration. People had been thrilled by the exploits of men such as Scott, Amundsen and Shackleton, who had become household names. Here again, in the dreary years that followed the war, was another great adventure to grip people's imaginations.

Curiously, Everest's frozen inaccessibility had led to it being commonly referred to as the "Third Pole". Now, this trip to the roof of the world – a spot so remote and dangerous that no one in the entire span of human history had even stood on its lower slopes, let alone its summit – was about to be played out before an eager public.

Not everyone welcomed the idea of an expedition. With almost every area of the globe explored and mapped, a few sceptics wondered whether there should be some small parts of the Earth left alone by man. Even those who were prepared to offer financial backing to such a trip wondered why they were doing it. There was "no more use in climbing Everest than kicking a football about, or dancing", said one eminent geographer. Still, he felt, such an extraordinary human achievement would "elevate the human spirit".

❖

In Britain in the early 1920s, the world of mountaineering was a rather select one. It was presided over by two distinguished organizations: the Royal Geographical Society and the Alpine Club. Between them, they set up an association known as the Everest Committee, to direct the climbing of the mountain.

At the time, climbing was a pastime only the rich could afford. Such men had been cut down in their thousands leading soldiers into battle in the First World War. Accordingly, the ranks of those suitable for an attempt on Everest had been thinned quite drastically.

So it was that the first expedition sent to explore Mount Everest was made up mainly of men in middle age. Those among them who had fought in the war had generally been too old or distinguished for the most dangerous front line service. The team leader, Lt. Col. Charles Howard-Bury, was a landowner in his late thirties. He had an impressive estate in Ireland and he bred race horses. A rather forbidding person, he was described by one of his team members as having "a very highly developed sense of hate and contempt for other sorts of people than his own". The head of the climbing team, a Scotsman named Harold Raeburn, was 56. Another colleague, a fellow Scot named Alexander Kellas, was 53 years old, and an expert on the effects of high altitude on the human body.

Also on the team were two younger men, Guy Bullock and George Mallory, who were 34 and 35 respectively. Both were gifted mountaineers, and they knew each other well. It was expected that they would do most of the serious climbing, and here Mallory established himself as the star of the team. A former school teacher who had served as an artillery officer during the war, he was tall, handsome and intelligent, and had a charisma unmatched by any other mountaineer before or since. "His limbs and all his movements were free and full of grace," said a friend, "and he had a strikingly beautiful face…"

Looking at Mallory as he peers from the grainy, mottled black and white photographs taken to record that first expedition, it is easy to see why he stood out. Among a forest of beards he is clean shaven, aside from a dashing moustache (which came and went). While his companions look distracted, crotchety and exhausted, Mallory stares into the camera, exuding strength and determination. The challenge of climbing Everest must have seemed a noble goal, well-suited to someone of such obviously heroic qualities. But there was another side to Mallory. While he was just the man with the guts and resolve to climb to the top of a previously unconquered mountain, he was also hopelessly impractical and forgetful – a shortcoming which would forever rule him out of leading an expedition.

❖

In May 1921, the team arrived in India, which was then part of the British empire. They assembled in Darjeeling, a city near the Himalayan mountains, where they recruited a team of porters to carry their equipment. Among this team were men and women from Nepal, known as Sherpas. Over the centuries, the Sherpas had supported themselves by trading, taking yaks laden with hides, grain, butter and textiles along steep mountain paths to other parts of Nepal, as well as India and Tibet, which had made them experts at transporting heavy loads at high altitudes. Right from the start, the Sherpas became an essential part of any expedition to the Himalayas.

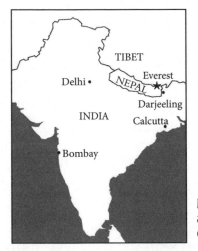

Almost immediately Howard-Bury's party

Map showing the countries around Everest at the time of the first expedition

was hit by ill-fortune. The trip to Everest was a long and difficult one, which required them to travel a dreary, dusty route through Tibet. Alexander Kellas, exhausted by the strain of the journey, and suffering from dysentery, died of a heart attack. Harold Raeburn was tormented by dire stomach pains caused by the poor food the team had brought along to eat. He had also fallen from his horse and been badly kicked, so was forced temporarily to abandon the expedition. Most of his colleagues were secretly pleased, for Raeburn had been an incompetent and irascible companion.

As Howard-Bury and his men were drawn towards Everest, they entered territory no westerner had ever visited before. They had literally "walked off the map", as Mallory described it. He wrote regularly to his wife Ruth, and their three young children, and in one memorable account he described his first proper view of Everest. Gazing at the distant peak through binoculars, the mountain was at first shrouded by mist. Then, "a whole group of mountains began to appear in gigantic fragments... like the wildest creation of a dream. A preposterous triangular lump rose out of the depths; its edge came leaping up at an angle of about 70 degrees and ended nowhere. Gradually, very gradually, we saw the great mountainsides and glaciers... until far higher in the sky than imagination had dared to suggest the white summit of Everest appeared."

Tibet is the highest country in the world, being,

on average, 4,900m (16,000ft) above sea level. As the men journeyed on, the high altitude began to take its toll. They all found themselves tiring quickly, as the thin air sapped their strength and stamina. "It is only possible to keep oneself going by remembering to puff like a steam-engine", Mallory wrote to his wife. Despite the exhausting work, the men's appetites seemed to have deserted them – this too was an effect of high altitude on the human body.

As they surveyed the territory around Everest, they could see that the mountain presented many possible routes to the top, but almost all of them looked dangerous and difficult. A massive three-sided pyramid, it was surrounded entirely by glaciers, as all great mountains are. Its three awesome faces were bisected by three great ridges of rock and ice – one to the South East, one to the North East and one to the West. The expedition decided that the North East Ridge reached via the North Col – a small snow-covered dip between the two peaks of Everest and nearby Changtse – looked like the surest way to the top.

❖

The highest the expedition got up Everest was the edge of the North Col, which stood 6,700m (22,000ft) above the East Rongbuk Glacier. But getting there completely exhausted most of Howard-Bury's men, who were constantly tormented by

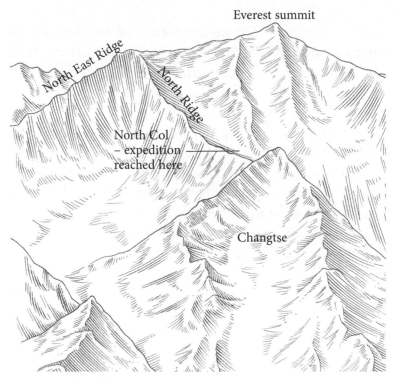

Everest showing the North Ridge and the North East Ridge

strong winds which prevented them from getting a proper night's sleep. Only Mallory wanted to press on to the top. But by then it was September and the Himalayan autumn was closing in fast. Howard-Bury wisely decided the expedition had done its job. They had taken a first close look at the mighty Everest from all sides, and now it was time to retreat and try again another year.

They had learned many useful lessons. Climbing Everest, it seemed, was a job more suited to younger

19

men – it required the kind of stamina and toughness that older men usually lacked. The climate around the mountain was fearsome, but the weather was best in May and early June, just before the arrival of the Monsoon, the formidable wind which brings rain and snow to Asia. Most of all, Howard-Bury's men established that high-altitude climbing was just as exhausting as they had expected. But, with the optimism of a nation whose empire controlled one quarter of the world, they were convinced that, with a little grit and determination, the summit was there for the taking.

Three more shots with "Bruiser" Bruce

The expedition of 1922

Such was the interest and excitement generated by Howard-Bury's trip that a second expedition was being planned even before the 1921 expedition had left India to return to Britain. Mallory, especially, seemed the focus of attention for the newspapers that followed the progress of the explorers. A lecture tour he undertook on his return also made his face better known to the public.

But despite its successes, Howard-Bury's team had been fractious and divided, largely because of the leader himself, who had taken a dislike to Mallory. So, behind the scenes at the National Geographic Society and Alpine Club, significant changes were planned for the 1922 expedition. A new leader was announced: General Charles Bruce, a genial, energetic bear of a man, known as "Bruiser" to his friends. A former officer in the British army's Gurkha regiment, he used to challenge soldiers from the regiment – tough but diminutive Nepalese men – to wrestle him four or five at a time. At 56, he was as old as many of the previous team, but he seemed a better choice of leader than his predecessor.

Of the 1921 expedition, only George Mallory and another climber named Henry Morshead remained. Other new climbers included Howard Somervell, Arthur Wakefield and Tom Longstaff. They were all doctors, although only Longstaff was brought along as the official team medic. Somervell, especially, was an extraordinary man. As well as being a gifted climber, he was a surgeon, a photographer, an artist and a musician, who would go on to write the score to a film about the early expeditions to Everest.

Another new team member was George Finch, an Australian who had been brought up in Switzerland. He was a notable climber who did much to pioneer modern mountaineering equipment. For example, he invented the down (feather-filled) jacket, which was considerably warmer than the wool and tweed most climbers then wore. Yet he was regarded as something of an upstart by the snootier British members of the expedition, and this undoubtedly prevented some of his good ideas from being accepted.

Also on the team were Edward Norton and Lt. Col. Edward Strutt, both distinguished climbers, and Charles Bruce's young cousin, Geoffrey Bruce. The younger Bruce had never climbed before in his life, but General Bruce thought he was the "right sort of chap" for an adventure like this. And along for the trip was expedition photographer Captain John Noel, who brought both still and movie cameras.

There was intense debate among the team as to whether or not they would use oxygen on the climb.

Recent laboratory experiments, using special chambers to simulate high altitudes, had shown that lack of oxygen in the air caused volunteers to become incapable of "controlled thinking and action" above 7,800m (26,000ft), and to slump into unconsciousness. Everest, it was noted, was at least 900m (3,000ft) higher than this. Finch had taken part in experiments which proved that oxygen would be extremely useful at such altitudes. But many climbers, Mallory especially, seemed to think that oxygen was "unsporting". There was even talk of climbers who used it being "rotters" – a schoolboy term, popular at the time, for cheats or otherwise disagreeable people.

But, despite its obvious advantages, there were two very good reasons not to use oxygen. Firstly, the metal tanks that held it had to be transported from "civilization" (in this case Darjeeling) to Everest. This added considerably to the weight of supplies. Secondly, a climber carrying an oxygen set of four tanks, a metal frame, and breathing apparatus, had an extra 15kg (33lb) to heave up the mountain – a weight equivalent to a heavy suitcase. "When I think of mountaineering with four cylinders of oxygen on one's back and a mask over one's face," said Mallory, "well, it loses its charm." In the end, a compromise was reached. Oxygen would be taken on the trip, but a climber could choose whether or not to use it.

There was another issue too, which was much discussed at the time, especially in the newspapers –

the possible existence on the mountain of a strange, ape-like creature called the Yeti. This report from *The Dundee Advertiser* is typical of some of the more overheated speculation about this mythical beast:

> Living among the perpetual snows of Mount Everest is a race of mystery men known in the Tibetan language as 'Abominable Snowmen', on account of their ferocity and the savage deeds they commit when they come into contact with the more or less civilized inhabitants of the region.

Fortunately, to this day, no one has ever been troubled by such a creature, but the newspapers' speculations must have been an added worry to the men about to scale the mountain.

❖

The team departed for the Himalayas at the end of March. The plan was for their expedition to be completed by mid-June, when the Monsoon was expected to start. By the end of April, they had reached the Rongbuk Valley, well on the way to Everest itself, and began to set up a string of camps at increasingly high altitudes. This tactic was known at the time as "the Polar method", because that was how Polar explorers had set about crossing the frozen wastes of the Arctic and Antarctic. Each camp would be a reasonable distance from the other, allowing a climber frequent stopping places on his route to the top. As a mountaineering technique, it worked so well that it is still used today by most expeditions on Everest and other high mountains.

General Bruce's plan of attack was to allow Mallory and Somervell a first attempt at the summit without oxygen. On May 10, they and a support team set off from Camp III for the North Col, the flat section of the mountain at the bottom of the North Ridge. This was a long backbone of rock that led directly to the North East Ridge, which divided the North and East faces of the mountain, and led, eventually, to the summit. The plan was to establish a camp here, as a staging post on the way to the top.

Most mountaineers begin to experience difficulty breathing above 5,790m (19,000ft). The North Col was 1,200m (4,000ft) higher. When they finally struggled up to it, the climbers found themselves utterly exhausted. They managed to put up five small green tents, but were so listless by the time they finished that they had to force themselves to eat. In order to combat loss of appetite, they had made a special effort to make their food as tempting as possible, hauling canned quail and champagne up the mountain. But no one had camped so high before, and the team soon realized high-altitude cooking brought with it special problems. Their loss of appetite was bad enough. But this high up, water boiled at a lower temperature, so the food they did not want to eat took much longer to cook. (Water normally boils at 100°C, but on the North Col it boils at only 80°C, so it takes around 14 times longer than usual to cook food there.)

When Strutt, the expedition second-in-command, reached the Col for the first time, he spluttered: "I wish that ****** cinema was here," (meaning Noel's movie camera). "If I look anything like what I feel, I ought to be immortalized for the British public."

From the North Col, a small group consisting of Mallory, Somervell, Norton and Morshead, together with four Sherpas, began their climb to the top. The plan was to establish another camp higher up, and rest there for the night. Then, the next day, they would head for the summit. They set off up the ridge on the morning of May 20, wearing their pith helmets, woolly jumpers and tweed jackets, with an optional scarf to ward off the cold. Quality clothes they may have been, but they were so preposterously unsuitable for Everest that mountaineers today still marvel at the courage and endurance of these early pioneers. They pressed on through a cruel wind, getting colder and more exhausted with every step. After three and a half hours, they had climbed a mere 600m (2,000ft) up the ridge. Eventually, at around two o'clock that afternoon, they found two ledges close together, which would be suitable spots for a couple of tents. Now they were no longer needed, the Sherpas were sent back to the North Col with instructions to return to Camp III, and the four climbers tried to rest and eat.

They set off again at eight o'clock the next morning, but almost at once Morshead confessed he didn't have the strength to continue. He returned to his tent, while the others carried on up the ridge. On they went, every step a massive effort, moving at less than 120m (400ft) an hour. Eventually, at around half past two that afternoon, they admitted defeat. But they had reached 8,169m (26,800ft) – higher than anyone had ever stood before.

Mallory, Somervell and Norton got back to their camp on the ridge, where Morshead was waiting, around four o'clock. As it was such a precarious spot, and they reasoned they would feel better lower down, they decided to head back to the North Col camp before darkness fell. This was a courageous decision. They were all utterly exhausted, and Morshead, especially, was no better for his rest.

The four men roped themselves together and descended through freshly fallen snow. Passing by the head of a gully, Morshead suddenly slipped, dragging Somervell and Norton down with him, and all three hurtled down the mountain. In an instant Mallory, who was leading the climb and had his back to his companions, heard them fall. He reacted with lightening speed, plunging his ice-axe into the deep snow and slipping the rope around it. Fortunately, the three falling men had not built up too much speed, and Mallory's quick thinking saved them all.

No one had been hurt in the fall, but all four were badly shaken. They moved down with even greater caution. Morshead became more of a problem. He was suffering from extreme exhaustion and frostbite – a particularly horrible condition where the flesh of the hands, toes or other prominent body parts freezes and can be irreparably damaged. He became irrational (a common symptom of high-altitude sickness), and kept on insisting that they slide down the mountain.

The decent slowed to a crawl and darkness overtook them. Then, to add to their alarming predicament, a storm brewed up in the west and lightning flashes lit their path. Eventually they reached the Col, but they were not safe yet. Several crevasses lay between them and their tents. They had only a crude candle lantern to light their way, and that burned out soon enough. Luckily, they stumbled on a rope that had earlier been fixed to a slope away from the Col, and this led them back to their tents.

It was now half past eleven at night, and the freezing climbers were desperate for food and a warm drink. But fate had played another trick on them. Due to a misunderstanding, the Sherpas had taken all the cooking equipment down to the camp below. The shivering men had to make do with an ice cream-like concoction of snow, condensed milk and strawberry jam. It was probably the last thing in the world they wanted to eat, and gave them all terrible stomach cramps throughout the night.

The lower altitude and a night's rest brought their strength back, and the four men were able to struggle back to Camp III the next day. Safe for the moment, all they wanted to do was drink warm tea. Somervell, it was recorded, drank 17 mugfulls. Morshead had recovered a little, but when the expedition returned to India in the summer, he had to have a toe and several fingers amputated. But, even as they returned down the mountain, they passed George Finch, Geoffrey Bruce and a team of Sherpas, heading up to the North Col with a generous supply of oxygen, all set for another attempt at the summit.

❖

Despite the extra weight they carried, Finch, Bruce and their team found climbing with oxygen much easier. Finch had also fashioned his own clothing. His down jacket, made from the kind of tough cloth used for hot-air balloons, had a quilted lining filled with eiderdown, and was much better suited to Everest than the flimsy clothing worn by the others. Armed with such advantages, he felt he had every chance of making the summit. Finch did worry about Bruce, though. This was the lad's first experience of mountaineering after all.

As they settled down for the night, the weather at the North Col grew worse. A terrible gale battered their tents and Finch recalled that the "wild flapping of the canvas made a noise like that of machine-gun fire". The wind was so savage the men had to shout to hear each other speak. But the next day the weather had settled slightly, and Finch and Bruce, now joined by another member of the party, a Gurkha named Tejbir Bura, headed up the mountain to make another camp along the North Ridge at 7,800m (25,500ft). The wind was so bad they feared their tents would be blown away. Here they stayed, gasping and wheezing in the thin air, their limbs growing numb with cold, for the night, the next day, and the next night. All of them could feel their strength ebbing away. But during the second night, Finch had a brilliant idea. He suggested they rig up their oxygen gear so they could breathe it while they rested. It worked like magic. Almost at once the freezing men felt stronger. Breathing oxygen also had the effect of making them feel warmer. All three slept well for the first time in days.

On May 24, at half past six in the morning, they emerged from their tent to begin their trek up to the summit. Tejbir collapsed soon afterwards, telling Finch and Bruce he had no strength to go on. Defeated, he returned to the tent. Then as Finch and Bruce climbed higher, a terrible wind blew up, making progress extremely slow. At 8,320m (27,300ft) disaster struck. Finch, who was leading the climb, suddenly heard Bruce call out in alarm: "I'm getting no oxygen!" Finch turned to see his companion wavering and about to topple off the mountain. He grabbed him, and they sat down together on a nearby ledge. Here Finch examined Bruce's oxygen set, discovered a broken glass tube, and quickly fixed it with a spare he was carrying. It had been a terrifying moment – at the time it was believed that a climber using oxygen at this height would die if his supply was cut off suddenly. This had proved not to be the case, but as Bruce began to breathe easily again, Finch decided the climb was over. Bruce, determined character that he was, wanted to go on, but the more experienced Finch realized that a nasty shock like this would sap his strength and morale. Despite a burning ambition to

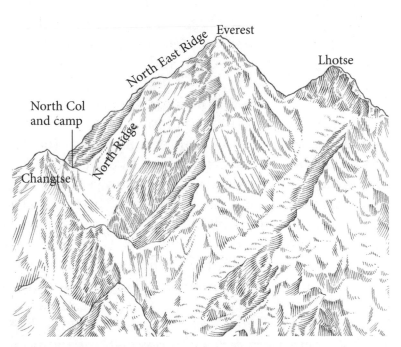

The northern approach to the summit

get to the summit, he decided to turn back before both of them fell to their deaths.

They headed down to Camp III, below the North Col, reaching it in a remarkably speedy 11 hours. Oxygen really did make climbing much easier. Despite their failure to reach the top, both men had climbed higher than anyone before – an especially remarkable achievement for Bruce on his first climb.

With two failed attempts behind them, and most of the climbers suffering from exhaustion or frostbite, the prospects for a third bid for the summit seemed slight. But Mallory was determined to go, and the expedition's backers in London were pressing for a result. It would be one attempt too many. It was now early June. The Monsoon, and the even harsher weather it would bring, would soon fall on the mountain. On June 5, Mallory, Somervell, another climber named Colin Crawford and 14 Sherpas headed up to the North Col. Around 200m (600ft) from the Col they heard a noise like an explosion shake the mountainside, and all were swept away by an avalanche. The British climbers had a lucky escape, but seven of the Sherpas were swept into a gaping crevasse. Everest had claimed its first victims.

The disaster brought the expedition to an abrupt end. Although photographer John Noel noted unkindly that the surviving Sherpas "had completely lost their nerve and were crying and shaking like babies", there were other climbers who were more compassionate. Somervell wrote: "why, oh why could not one of us Britishers have shared their fate? I would gladly at that moment have been lying there dead in the snow, if only to give those fine chaps who had survived the feeling that we shared their loss, as we had indeed shared the risk."

Mallory blamed himself for the accident, despite the fact that the whole team had decided on the route to the Col. It was a sad end to an extraordinary expedition. Yet, despite the dangers and this disaster, success had been almost within their grasp. Another expedition would surely succeed…

"More like war than mountaineering"

The 1924 expedition

There was no expedition in 1923. Funds were low, changes to equipment had to be made and the right people were not available. In 1924, however, a new expedition set off with the usual fanfare of articles in the papers. *The Newcastle Journal* even carried this extraordinary claim:

> Smoking largely contributed to the success of last year's ascent and members declared that Mount Everest would have been completely scaled had not their supplies given out at 27,300ft [8,190m] above sea level.

In our health-conscious age, the thought of wheezing, breathless mountaineers having a cigarette on the giddy slopes near the summit seems unthinkable. But in 1924, it was seriously believed that smoking helped a climber to breathe better and fight fatigue.

"Bruiser" Bruce had proved to be such a good leader on the last trip, he was the obvious choice again, despite his increased age (he was now 58) and shaky health. Edward Norton, another veteran from the 1922 trip, would be his second-in-command. Mallory was asked again too. His renown had landed him a prestigious teaching job in Cambridge and he had only recently moved there with his family, but the Everest Committee wanted him back – he was, after all, their most famous climber. Mallory was beset with doubt. On the previous trip, he had noted "frankly the game (of climbing the mountain) is not good enough... the risks of getting caught are too great... and the margin of strength when men are at such great heights is too small". He was torn between his wife and children, and his ambition to reach the summit of Everest and the duty he felt to his fellow mountaineers. Just before he left England, he told a friend: "This is going to be more like war than mountaineering. I don't expect to come back."

Also along from the previous trip were Howard Somervell, Geoffrey Bruce and John Noel and his cameras. Among the new men (there was no question, in 1924, of women joining the team) was a geologist and experienced climber named Noel Odell, and a young, fair-haired engineering student from Oxford University, named Andrew "Sandy" Irvine. He had little climbing experience, but had shown himself to be a great team player and determined explorer in a recent expedition to the Arctic. On top of this, he was a brilliant mechanic. General Bruce overlooked his lack of experience in the light of all his other obvious qualities. Irvine was a good choice – he was well liked by the team, and adapted quickly to the high-altitude life.

The expedition left Darjeeling on March 25, intending to head up the Rongbuk Glacier and again take the North Col route to the summit. But within two weeks General Bruce had succumbed to malaria, and had to return to Darjeeling. Norton took over. He had been well chosen, and was liked and respected by his team. On the way there, as Everest loomed into view, final plans were made. The climbers were optimistic. Mallory, his doubts now replaced by an iron determination, even wrote to his wife: "It is almost unthinkable... that I shan't get to the top; I can't see myself coming down defeated." He would turn out to be right in some respects – but not in the way he hoped.

❖

The expedition reached Rongbuk on April 28 but, almost immediately, bad weather hampered its progress. Two Sherpas died of frostbite and high-altitude sickness. Then, in the middle of May, heavy snow forced them to abandon the camp they had established on the North Col. During the retreat four Sherpas, too terrified to come down, had been left at the camp. Norton, Mallory and Somervell had to form a rescue party to bring them to safety.

At the end of May the weather improved, but time was rapidly running out. The annual Monsoon would soon bring more snow, so an all-out assault on the summit was quickly mounted. Camps were established again at the North Col, and at two spots up the North Ridge. This final stopping point, known as Camp VI, was only 600m (2,000ft) from the summit. But above it lay some of the most difficult conditions and obstacles of the climb. In the teeth of whatever weather the mountain might throw at them, a climber would have to make his way through a yellow band of slippery, crumbling slabs of rock, which overlapped like roof tiles. After that, they faced a 30m (100ft) wall of rock known as the "First

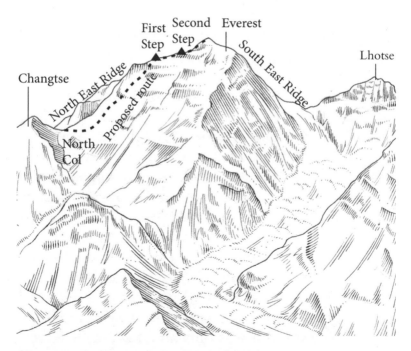

The route via the First and Second Steps

Step". Then, there was a difficult passage up a narrow ridge to another 30m (100ft) wall of rock known as the "Second Step". This was a particularly nasty looking obstacle, which looked like "the sharp bow of a battlecruiser". After that, there was a relatively easy climb up the final peak to the summit. But anyone who struggled up there would have to come down in a state of total exhaustion. It was not going to be easy.

Norton decided that he and Somervell should make the first attempt at the summit and that they would not use oxygen. On June 4, at twenty to seven in the morning, the pair set off from their tent at Camp VI in perfect weather. The high altitude caused immediate problems. Somervell developed a bad sore throat and had difficulty breathing. Norton had forgotten his sunglasses, and soon suffered snow glare so badly he had double vision. Despite this, these two men pressed on through the morning. They planned their route to pass around the two difficult Steps. This would make for a longer climb, but would be safer. Both were making extremely slow progress, and could only move forward 12 or 13 steps before they had to stop to get their breath back.

By midday Somervell could carry on no longer, and sat down to rest on a ledge. Norton pressed on through deep snow for a while, reaching a record height of 8,650m (28,200ft), just below the final stretch. The summit was only about 240m (800 feet) above. But he knew that if he continued, he would never return. Feeling a curious mixture of disappointment and relief, Norton rejoined Somervell, and the two made their way back to Camp VI. Somervell later wrote: "We had been willing always to risk our lives, but we did not believe in throwing them away."

❖

After a brief stop at Camp VI, Norton led off down to the North Col. Then behind him, Somervell had a violent coughing fit, and all of a sudden he couldn't breathe. He couldn't even call out to Norton to help him, and sat down in the snow to die. In a last desperate effort, he pressed hard on his chest and coughed up a huge lump of mucus. Despite being in a great deal of pain, Somervell could breathe again. He felt elated. His narrow escape from death filled him with a fresh energy, and the climbers returned safely to Camp IV. But during the night Norton felt an intense pain in his eyes, and went completely blind for the next 60 hours.

On his return, Norton was convinced that the expedition was over. But as he lay in his tent, draped with sleeping bags to keep out any light, Mallory came to him with plans for a final summit attempt. This time, said Mallory, they would use oxygen. He persuaded Norton, who wrote of him: "I… was full of admiration for the indomitable spirit of the man… in spite of his already excessive exertions, not to admit defeat while any chance remained." There was one point of disagreement, however. Mallory had formed a close friendship with Irvine, and wanted to take him as a climbing partner. Norton felt the more experienced Noel Odell would be a wiser choice. But sick and exhausted as he was, he did not have the strength to argue.

❖

On June 6, Mallory, Irvine and a small team of Sherpas headed up the mountain. The next day the two climbers reached Camp VI, where they slept overnight. Mallory wrote a final message to photographer John Noel, which was carried down to the North Col by the Sherpas, who all returned down the mountain that evening. It said:

Dear Noel,

We'll probably start early tomorrow (8th) in order to have clear weather. It won't be too early to start looking for us either crossing the rock band or going up the skyline at 8:00pm.

Yours ever,
G. Mallory

The "pm" was an obvious mistake, no doubt caused by exhaustion. But the note seemed to indicate that Mallory was intending to go the quickest, most direct route to the summit, through the difficult terrain of the First and Second Steps, rather than trying to bypass these obstacles, as Norton and Somervell had done.

Sure enough, Mallory and Irvine set off for the top of Everest the following morning. For Irvine this was a great adventure, and he was thrilled to be climbing with the legendary Mallory. Perhaps Norton had been wrong to worry about Irvine, for he had proved to be both a fast and capable climber. For Mallory, this attempt was far more serious. He was nearly 38 years old. He had failed to reach the summit on two previous occasions. Supplies were running low, the climbers and Sherpas were exhausted, and the Monsoon was almost upon them. This was surely his last chance, and he was determined to succeed or die.

Also heading up the mountain that morning was the expedition geologist Noel Odell. He had spent the night at Camp V on the North Col and was climbing through a thin mist up to Camp VI, with some supplies Mallory had requested for their return journey.

Odell was delighted to come across some fossils on his way up the mountain. As he pottered, he reached a small ledge around 7,925m (26,000ft). There, at around one o'clock, a mist above him lifted, and he could see right up to the summit. High above, he spotted two tiny specks around the area of the First or Second Step. He was surprised they were so low

41

on their way to the summit, at this point in the day, but noticed they were moving at good speed.

Around two o'clock that afternoon, the weather changed dramatically and a howling wind whipped up a snow storm. Odell, anxious that the returning climbers would lose their way back to the camp, ventured away from the tent and up into the storm, whistling and yodelling as he went, hoping Mallory and Irvine might be listening. But no one was there to hear him.

❖

Mallory had given Odell clear instructions not to stay at Camp VI – there was room for only two climbers in the tent. So when the storm lifted around four o'clock and bright sunshine flooded the mountainside, he retreated to the North Col, after having a final look around for the two men.

Above him, roped together, Mallory and Irvine were struggling. The storm had knocked the strength from their already failing, frozen limbs, and they were fighting for their lives, hoping to return to the shelter of Camp VI before darkness. To add to their troubles, the climb had taken far longer than they planned. Their oxygen had run out, and both had now discarded their heavy breathing apparatus. Having to manage without oxygen at this stage of the climb, when they were desperately in need of all the strength they could summon, was a terrible blow.

As dusk fell, they edged slowly to safety. But they had still not reached the campsite when a moonless night fell upon them. Above Camp VI, perhaps no more than half an hour's climb away, one of them stumbled and fell, dragging his companion behind him. Somewhere on the fall the rope between them snapped. Mallory plunged down the steep North Face, breaking his right leg in two places as he fell. Fighting desperately to save his life, he dug his fingers into the scree, ripping his gloves off in the process. But before he came to a halt he was jerked into the air, and his head hit a sharp rock.

Mallory often thought of his children when he climbed, and perhaps he thought of them then as he lay still, face down on the side of the mountain, crossing his left leg over his broken right in an effort to ease the pain, his fingers digging into the small gravel stones of the slope that would be his final resting place.

Irvine had been injured too, but not as badly as Mallory. He probably dragged himself back up the slope, determined to reach the life-saving oxygen supplies and warmth of his tent. But somewhere in his search for shelter, the second-year Oxford student, who was all of 22, collapsed and died.

❖

Their companions below had no means of knowing what had happened. All through the evening Odell kept an anxious watch on the slopes, but saw nothing either to worry or reassure him. The following morning he took two Sherpas as far as Camp V, but it was too cold to go further.

The next day was June 10. Although the Sherpas refused to go any higher, Odell hauled himself up to Camp VI alone to look for his missing comrades. Ominously, the tent there looked exactly the same as when he had left it two days before. He searched long, hard and heroically, thinking as he did so that "this upper part of Everest must... be the remotest and most inhospitable spot on Earth". Of Mallory and Irvine there was no trace.

There was now little doubt in Odell's mind that they had been killed. His strength ebbing, he returned to the tent and laid the sleeping bags out in the shape of a T – a pre-arranged signal to his companions below that the two climbers were missing. As he gingerly made his way down to the North Col, he glanced over his shoulder at the looming, distant summit. "It seemed to look down with cold indifference on me," he later wrote, "and howl derision in wind-gusts at my petition to yield up its secrets – the mystery of my friends."

Back at the North Col, Odell had yet another signal to relay to Norton and other colleagues at the base of the mountain – six blankets laid out in the shape of a cross. This was a confirmation that Irvine and Mallory were dead. The expedition was over. Before they left the mountain, Somervell and the others built a memorial cairn of stones and slate on a spot overlooking Base Camp. On the slate they recorded the names of the 12 people who had died during the expeditions of 1921, 1922 and 1924. As the century wore on, there would be plenty more names to follow them.

Although their attempts to reach the summit of Everest had ended in tragedy, there was much to admire about these early pioneers. Dressed in tweed jackets and woolly jumpers, they looked, in the words of playwright George Bernard Shaw, "like a picnic in Connemara surprised by a snowstorm". Yet Norton, on the second summit attempt, and maybe Mallory and Irvine after him, had reached a height on Everest that would not be bettered for nearly 30 years.

❖

Norton sent a terse telegram back to London –

```
Mallory and Irvine killed on
last attempt. Rest of party
arrived   at   Base   Camp   all
well.
```

Ruth Mallory's telegram from the Everest Committee was a little less brusque –

```
Committee    deeply    regret
received  bad  news  Everest
expedition    today.    Your
husband  and  Irvine  killed
last climb...
```

In the spirit of the times, Ruth Mallory took the news with a controlled dignity. She wrote to a friend: "whether he got to the top of the mountain or did not, whether he lived or died, makes no difference to my admiration for him… (yet) if only it hadn't happened! It so easily might not have." But for months afterwards, it was said, she looked like "a stately lily with its head broken and hanging down".

The news was announced in *The Times* on June 21, 1924. Mallory and Irvine's deaths caused a sensation in the English-speaking world. *The London Sunday Express*, for example, declared the tragedy "a great and heroic story of adventure, courage and fate…" A picture of Irvine in his college blazer appeared in many papers. He looked barely more than a boy. His obituary in *The Alpine Journal* (the Alpine Club's annual review) carried a sentimental poem from a teacher at his old school: "God and the stars alone could see thee die…"

Later that year, a memorial service for the two climbers was held at St Paul's Cathedral in London. Even the Royal family sent representatives.

❖

There was much speculation as to whether or not the two ill-fated climbers had reached the summit. Arguments that they might not have made it were rather overlooked in a tide of sentimentality. Those who were friends of Mallory's, especially, were convinced he had made it to the summit. One of the 1922 team wrote: "… they got there alright… how they must have appreciated the view of half the world; it was worthwhile to them; now they'll never grow old."

No doubt the thought that Mallory and Irvine had succeeded made their friends feel their "sacrifice" had had some purpose. But expedition leader Edward Norton was more level-headed. There was no proof, he said, so no one could say for certain. The Everest Committee agreed with him. As far as they were concerned, Everest had still to be climbed.

Although the names of Mallory and Irvine remain a legend to mountaineers, their fame has faded over the years. Today, Mallory does not even rate a mention in most biographical encyclopedias or dictionaries – yet at the time of his death, he was regarded as one of the greatest heroes of his age. It was Mallory, when asked why he wanted to climb Everest, who gave the famous response, "Because it's there."

"A lifetime of fear and struggle"

The expedition of 1933

It would be nine years before another Everest expedition set out. Tibet's spiritual leader, the Dalai Lama, had been perturbed by all the deaths on the mountain, and British government officials, wanting to keep him as an ally, had forbidden further attempts. Then, in 1929, the world was hit by the Great Depression. As businesses and banks collapsed and unemployment soared, funding climbing trips was not regarded as a high priority.

It was not until 1933 that the Everest Committee was able to clear the way for another expedition – both in terms of raising funds and gaining official permission to climb the mountain. Their determination to continue was prompted partly by other countries badgering the British Government for a try at Everest. The British had used their influence in the region most unfairly to forbid any other nation from climbing the mountain. But the Germans, Swiss and Americans who wanted to try for the summit could not be deterred forever.

Before the British could launch another attempt, they had to recruit a new team. The 1924 climbers had mainly been middle-aged men. Now, nearly a decade on, most would be too old for another trip. A distinguished ex-Indian civil service commissioner, Hugh Ruttledge, was appointed as leader. At 48, he was quite old for mountaineering, and had very little climbing experience. But he had a good knowledge of the Himalayas and the local people there, and was considered to be "the right sort of chap".

The team assembled around him was an extremely strong one. There was Eric Shipton, only 25 and already an experienced and respected mountaineer. Others, such as Percy Wyn Harris, Jack Longland and Lawrence Wager, also had fine reputations. Most well-known and interesting of all was the successful writer and photographer, Frank Smythe. Hardly a likeable character, photographs of Smythe show a frail, irascible-looking man, with sharp, almost feminine features. He could be difficult company, but his prickly exterior hid a personality at war with itself. He was convinced others were stronger and cleverer than him, but was determined to push himself to the limits of his abilities, so no one would ever know. This was just the sort of drive and determination that might get a man to the summit.

❖

Despite its new members, Ruttledge's expedition was little different from the last one. All the climbers came from the same well-to-do social background, their equipment was much the same, and the route they chose to follow was also directly the same as before. But there were two significant differences. Firstly, the Sherpas, with almost 15 years of climbing experience now behind them, had become first-class mountaineers. In the absence of British expeditions, they had climbed other Himalayan peaks with American, German and Swiss teams. Secondly, new equipment was available.

Unlike earlier expeditions, Ruttledge's men brought radio sets with them. Although radio had become an established technology during the First World War, the sets had been too bulky and unreliable to bother carrying up a mountain. But by 1933, radio sets had become much more portable (although by modern standards they were still pretty big, and each needed six large acid batteries to power it). Radio brought obvious advantages. Ruttledge, via relay stations, could send news of their progress to the Everest Committee in London within a day. And by radio, the team could receive advance warning of the arrival of the fearful Monsoon.

In the years since the last expedition, there had also been a major advance in the design of oxygen equipment, and oxygen sets now weighed only 5.75kg (12.75lbs), just over a third of the weight of the old sets. But although the team decided to bring oxygen with them, they were determined not to use it. Opinions on oxygen were still heated, and many people felt its use was "unsporting". One of the climbers on the 1933 trip likened it to using a motor in a yachting race.

❖

The team set up their base camp at Rongbuk Glacier on April 17. Almost at once, appalling weather dogged them. As they assembled for their customary team photographs, Ruttledge must have wondered how many of his men would live to see the summer back home in England.

They sheltered from the storms as best they could, but then illness swept through the party. Flu, upset stomachs, bronchitis, even a gastric ulcer, weakened a team that was facing the most demanding physical challenge of their lives. Eventually, the weather improved. On May 14, almost a month after they had arrived, they set up a camp on the North Col. Like all previous camps on the Col, it was dubbed No. IV.

No sooner had they set up the camp than news came via the radio that that year's Monsoon had already reached Ceylon (now called Sri Lanka). They probably had less than two weeks before worsening weather would make climbing impossible. But even before the Monsoon's arrival, the weather was dreadful. Storms brought the ferrying of supplies up the mountain to a halt for five days between May 16 and May 20. At the camp on the foot of the Col, tents were felled by the wind and men almost froze to death. But there was worse to come.

In the gaps between the storms, the climbers managed to set up a Camp V at 7,620m (25,000ft) up the North Ridge. Then, on May 29, at 8,440m (27,700ft), a single tent made up Camp VI. This would be the final stopping-off spot for two climbers before the summit. It was placed precariously on a ledge so thin that a quarter of the tent hung over the North Face of the mountain. The Monsoon was expected any day. If anyone was going to get to the top, they had very little time left to do it.

Ruttledge had decided the two climbers to make the first attempt at the summit would be Percy Wyn-Harris and Lawrence Wager. They, along with Jack Longland and eight Sherpas, had set up Camp VI. As Wyn-Harris and Wager settled down to rest, Longland returned down the mountain with the Sherpas around one o'clock in the afternoon. The trip up to Camp VI had been exhausting. The climbers, all carrying equipment for the camp, had to stop for three or four breaths between each step. Now, on the way down, they were all dangerously tired, so Longland decided to take them directly down the top of the North Ridge. It was not the quickest route, but it was the safest.

The weather that afternoon was so clear Longland stopped briefly to admire the view. He recalled seeing "peaks that must have been more than 250 miles [400 km] away" – an amazing distance to see, roughly equivalent to the distance between London and Plymouth, or Los Angeles and San Francisco. But then, suddenly, his party was hit by a storm which sprang from nowhere. Snow quickly filled the holds on the rocks and made the scree beneath their feet treacherous. The wind blew so hard, said Longland, that the men could do little but "cling and cower against the rocks".

The North Ridge had been a gamble. It was safer, but Longland did not know it well. As the snow froze on his goggles, obscuring his already limited view, he tore them from his face, only to have his eyelashes and eyelids freeze up instead. Slowly, slowly, they edged down the mountain, stopping every ten minutes to make sure all nine of them were still together. Then, ahead, they saw a tent. Amazingly, they had stumbled upon Mallory and Irvine's Camp VI, unoccupied for the last nine years. Despite their terrible plight, Longland and the Sherpas could not resist a quick look around. In the tent, there was a flashlight which was still in working order.

But this was not a good time to hunt for souvenirs. Besides, when they discovered the tent, Longland began to wonder if they were seriously lost. He thought he knew where Mallory and Irvine's Camp VI was on the mountain, but it was not on the route they were supposed to be taking. Nearby were steep, overhanging ice cliffs, that plunged right down to the East Rongbuk Glacier. In a storm, when visibility was almost zero, this was not a good place to be. Longland kept these thoughts to himself, not wanting the Sherpas to lose their faith in his leadership, but the next half hour was a nightmare. At any second, Longland expected one of his team to slip in the blizzard and plunge down a slippery slope, over the cliff to certain death thousands of feet below.

They pressed on for another half hour. By now, some of the Sherpas were so exhausted that they sat down in the snow. Longland was losing confidence fast, and wondered whether it would be better for everyone just to lie down and die quietly from exposure, rather than be killed in a violent fall after hours of struggle. But he was determined not to give up while there was still hope. Pulling the stragglers to their feet, he urged them all on down the mountain. Eventually, he later recalled, "down through the snow… appeared a little patch of green. I rubbed the ice off my eyelashes and looked again: and it was a tent, three, four tents – the little cluster that meant Camp V and safety, and an end to the tearing anxiety of two hours." Reflecting on his experience, Longland wrote, "I seemed to have crowded a lifetime of fear and struggle and responsibility into that short time." So far, at least, the 1933 expedition had survived without fatalities.

❖

Meanwhile, up at Camp VI, Percy Wyn-Harris and Lawrence Wager sat out the storm that had so nearly claimed the lives of nine of their companions. They rested as best they could at such an exhausting altitude, then set off for the summit the next morning at twenty to six – before the dawn. Their goal lay a mere 490m (1,600ft) above them. Their strategy was to follow Mallory and Irvine's supposed route up the difficult rock faces of the First and Second Steps – the most direct route to the top.

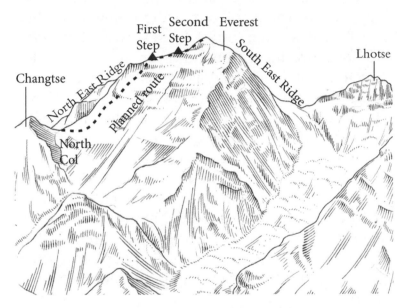

The planned route via the First and Second Steps

An hour into the climb, and shortly after dawn, Wyn-Harris found an ice-axe. It could only be Mallory or Irvine's, for no other men had walked this way. But when Wyn-Harris and Wager approached the First Step, they abandoned their plan. It looked too steep and difficult. Instead, they decided to do what Edward Norton and Howard Somervell had done in 1924, and try to reach Everest's final summit cone by going around the Steps. This route was longer, but it was safer.

They retraced Norton and Somervell's steps in more ways than one. After passing though the yellow band of rock that lies just below the summit cone, they came to a gully full of powdery snow. It was half past twelve and the top of Everest was all of 300m (900ft) above them. But however much they were driven by ambition, Wyn-Harris and Wager had every intention of returning home alive. They reckoned on another four hours of climbing before they reached the top, almost all of it through snow. It would be exhausting and dangerous, but not half as dangerous as the return journey. This late in the day there would be no chance of getting back to Camp VI by nightfall, and they would almost certainly die on the way down. Feeling more relief than disappointment, they turned back. They had reached almost exactly the same height as Edward Norton had done in 1924.

But even as they returned to the precarious haven of Camp VI, another two climbers were heading up the mountain. Frank Smythe and Eric Shipton were both extremely capable and determined men. They knew each other well and had made many difficult climbs together. Perhaps they were the men who would find a way to the summit...

Their summit day did not start well. It was so cold

on the morning of June 1, they could not leave their tent until half past seven – a very late start for the difficult climb ahead. Like their companions before them, they originally intended to climb the First and Second Steps. But as they drew nearer, these steep cliffs seemed too difficult to handle.

There were other problems too. Both men had been high up on the mountain for several days, and Shipton, especially, was feeling the effects of altitude sickness. Just as they reached the First Step he collapsed and decided he could go no further. After a brief consultation they decided that Shipton would return to Camp VI, and Smythe would press on to the summit alone. It was an extraordinarily brave decision, for Smythe was also suffering from the high-altitude sickness that had overwhelmed Shipton.

In a state of near-collapse, he soon began to feel he was accompanied by another climber – a sensation familiar to lone desert and polar explorers in a similar state of exhaustion. Smythe even believed he and his invisible friend were roped together: "If I slipped, 'he' would hold me," he recalled. When Smythe stopped to rest and took out some mint cake (an energy-giving sweet), he even turned around to offer his friend some.

But Smythe's solo attempt was doomed to failure. When he reached 8,600m (28,200ft), only 240m (800ft) up to the summit, he encountered a lethal obstruction. Ahead was a gully which Smythe later recounted with his writer's gift for vivid description: "Snow had accumulated deeply [on the] ledges... soft like flour, loose like granulated sugar and incapable of holding the feet in position. As I probed it with my axe I knew the game was up."

Struggling for breath, his body starved of oxygen, he found he completely lacked the willpower to carry on. Maybe, just maybe, if such gifted climbers had taken the new, lighter oxygen sets, they would have found the energy and determination to reach the summit. As it was, no one would stand higher on the mountain than Smythe had done, that June day in 1933, for almost another 20 years.

The actual route of the 1933 expedition

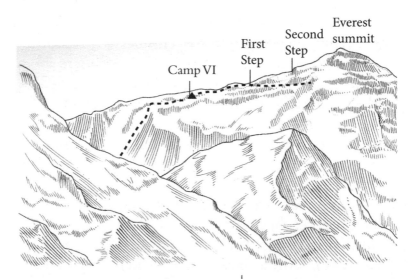

The journey back to Camp VI was a bizarre one. Still accompanied by his invisible friend, Smythe began to pick his way carefully down the mountain. At around 8,200m (27,000ft), when he was 60m (200ft) from the camp, he had the most vivid hallucination. As he later wrote: "chancing to glance in the direction of the North Ridge, I saw two curious-looking objects floating in the sky. They strongly resembled kite-balloons in shape, but one possessed what appeared to be squat, under-developed wings, and the other a protuberance suggestive of a beak. They hovered motionless but seemed slowly to pulsate, a pulsation much slower than my own heart-beats... The two objects were very dark... and were silhouetted sharply against the sky."

Smythe took in this extraordinary vision with a detached curiosity. As well as checking that these mystery objects were pulsating at a different rate than his own pulse, he also noted that they did not move when he moved his eyes swiftly away from them. Whatever they were, they seemed to be disconnected from his own body. This became even more apparent when he looked away and then back again, and they were still in the same spot in the sky where they had been before. Eventually a mist drifted in front of them. When the mist cleared, they were gone.

Smythe thought he had seen "some strange effect of mist and mountain magnified by imagination. On the other hand, it may have been a mirage." Since then, other more fanciful writers have claimed that what Smythe had seen was an Unidentified Flying Object, or UFO. However, it is much more likely that it was an hallucination brought about by lack of oxygen and exhaustion. Whatever the objects really were, Smythe's story – along with stories about the Yeti – contributed further to Everest's air of mystery.

❖

Back at Camp VI Smythe rejoined Shipton, who had recovered from his earlier breakdown. Exhausted, Smythe collapsed and slept until the next day. As the tent was so uncomfortable, Shipton decided to head down the mountain to Camp V before nightfall. Smythe came down the next morning. By chance, both men were caught in sudden storms like the one that had caused Longland and his eight Sherpas such trouble. Flattened against rocks by intense winds, or almost lifted off their feet, they had to cower behind boulders and in crevices, and then dash forward between squalls. This was the year when climbers learned that Everest could have terrible weather in May and early June, even before the Monsoon arrived. But despite the weather, everyone on Hugh Ruttledge's expedition survived.

Looking back on the climb, Smythe wrote tellingly of the hardship he and his comrades had endured: "Toil, discomfort, freezing cold and burning sun, failing appetite, sleeplessness, irritation, boredom, these are some of the penalties of Everest." Of the approach to the summit he recalled: "What a feeble instrument the body is at 28,000ft [8,500m]. A man who climbs near the top of Everest is a poor dull creature, barely existing in a grey world devoid of pleasure... he seems to tread some shadowy line between consciousness and unconsciousness, between, indeed, life and death." Yet Smythe also wrote of "nature at her noblest and most beautiful", and spoke of the breath-taking sights he had witnessed near the summit, looking "past the specks of the Rongbuk Monastery and away over the golden plains of Tibet, where the wandering clouds were couched on their own shadows, to the blue distance where the earth bent over into the fastness of central Asia".

The reckless Yorkshireman

Maurice Wilson's solo attempt

The papers were full of Everest in the spring of 1933 – not only had Hugh Ruttledge's expedition caught the imagination of the public, but a plane flight over the mountain had also attracted considerable interest. Someone paying very close attention was Maurice Wilson.

Born in Bradford, Yorkshire, in 1898, Wilson had had an unhappy end to his adolescence and this had shaped the rest of his life. Like most British men born in the last decade of the 19th century, he was destined for the carnage of the First World War. Wilson had enlisted as soon as he reached 18, and had found himself, while not yet out of his teens, fighting in the mud of Passchendaele – one of the most hideous battles of the war. His bravery won him the Military Cross, but he was hit by machine gun fire across the chest and left arm. He recovered, but his arm was never the same again.

Many men who survived the intense excitement and terror of the war found the humdrum reality of life back home difficult to take. Wilson was among them. He married, but soon divorced and moved to the United States, and then to New Zealand. Although he had made money and was quite prosperous, he never settled at anything. His 30th birthday came and went, and still he hadn't found a niche in life.

Suffering from depression, he came home. On the boat back to England from New Zealand, he met some Indian holy men who made a great impression on him. He developed a personal philosophy based on both Christianity and Indian meditation. Back in England, he continued to suffer from bouts of depression, and his health deteriorated alarmingly. But after a regime of prayer, and fasting almost to the point of starvation, he managed to make a full recovery. The success of his new philosophy convinced him that people could do anything if they had enough faith and determination. He decided, at the age of 33, that his mission in life was to spread this message to his fellow humans.

He could preach on street corners, and even book town and village halls to spread his teachings, but he recognized that this would almost certainly result in indifference or humiliation. Wilson was canny enough to realize that the best advertisement for his new philosophy would be a feat of daring that would astound the world. What better place to start than a solo climb up the world's highest, and so far unclimbed, mountain? As he said at the time: "When I have accomplished my little work, I shall be somebody. People will listen to me..."

His plan of action was remarkably simple. He would fly to India and then to the Himalayas, where he would crash-land a plane as high up the mountain as it would go. (Most planes in 1933 did not have the power to fly over a peak as high as Everest.) Then he would trek on foot to the top.

The fact that he could not fly and had never been up a mountain made his plan both alarmingly stupid and enormously brave. Wilson was the ultimate "can-do" kind of man, much of his confidence stemming from his own imposing frame (he was well over 6ft tall) and physical strength. He enrolled at the London Aero Club for flying lessons, and went hiking in the rugged moorland of the English Lake District, to give himself a grasp of mountaineering. To build up his stamina, he regularly walked from his home in London to his parents' house in Bradford – a distance of some 420km (260 miles).

Following his flying lessons, he bought himself a second-hand Gypsy Moth – a dinky single-seater biplane which he fitted with long-distance fuel tanks and named, punningly, "Ever-Wrest". By the spring of 1933 he was all set to go, and flew up to his parents in Bradford to say goodbye. But crossing over Yorkshire, he crashed the plane into farmland. He survived unscathed, but patching up "Ever-Wrest" added another three weeks to his departure date. By now, Wilson's designs on Everest had made him a familiar face in the British press, who had dubbed him "The Mad Yorkshireman". "He got small photographs in the newspapers, as a man might who announced his intentions of swimming the Atlantic with water-wings", one obituary rather snootily recalled later.

As Wilson prepared to depart from Stag Lane Aerodrome in Edgware, North London, a telegram from the British Air Ministry arrived forbidding him to leave. With a magnificent lack of respect, Wilson tore it up and took to the air. Within a week he was in Cairo, and a week after that he had arrived in India. The mighty wrath of the British government followed him all the way – forbidding him fuel at some stops, and not allowing him to fly over some countries on his route. Yet in 1933, the fact that an inexperienced pilot could make such a journey and survive was a magnificent achievement in itself. His flight gained him a great deal of publicity. Ironically, Wilson had created exactly the kind of impact he had wanted, even before he reached the Himalayas.

❖

Once in India, then part of the British empire, Wilson's plane was impounded and he was refused permission to fly over both Tibet and Nepal. Forced to modify his plans, he decided to sell the Gypsy Moth (which the authorities allowed him to do) and walk to Darjeeling – the Indian city nearest to the Himalayas. All this made it impossible to consider an ascent of Everest that year. By the time Wilson was ready to go, the Monsoon had arrived. So he sat out the rest of the year, living off the proceeds from his Gypsy Moth and training for the ascent on a diet of dates and cereals, coupled with bouts of fasting and deep breathing practice.

It was difficult even for expeditions with the full backing of the prestigious Royal Geographical Society and Alpine Club to get permission to climb Everest. Maurice Wilson had no chance of getting permission at all. But this was not going to deter him. In early 1934, he hired three Sherpas and walked into Tibet disguised as a monk, often moving only at night. By April 1934, he had reached the Rongbuk Glacier, the usual starting point for an ascent up the North Ridge – the only route by which it was thought possible to reach the summit. Here, he met the head monk at the monastery at Rongbuk, who was greatly impressed by this strange Englishman and his spiritual crusade.

On April 16, weighed down with a 20kg (45lb) rucksack, he left his Sherpas behind at his Base Camp and set off alone to conquer Everest. He knew which way to go, as he had studied the accounts of previous expeditions. But he had no real grasp of the extreme difficulties involved in Himalayan climbing, nor did he have any of the necessary equipment for climbing safely in snow and ice. Even when he had the good luck to find a discarded pair of crampons, spiked metal footwear essential for climbing in ice, he didn't bother to attach them to his boots. He kept a detailed journal of his trip, and recorded each day's activity with boyish enthusiasm...

April 20: Still about 2½ miles [4km] to go to Camp III when shall look forward to some hot chocolate.

April 21: 36 today. Many happy returns to myself... hellish cold but alright.

April 22: ... no use going on – eyes horrible and throat dry.

Wilson returned after nine days in a state of utter exhaustion, with a sore throat brought on by altitude sickness, and his war wounds hurting badly. He had been plagued by terrible snow storms, and had not even reached the top of the glacier. He was lucky not to have died of exposure.

After an 18-day rest, he felt strong enough to try again, wisely taking two of his Sherpas with him. They knew the best way through the crevasses and ice blocks of the glacier, and this time they reached the foot of Everest in a mere three days. The three men set up camp beneath the North Col, but were immediately trapped in their tents by fierce blizzards, and suffered terribly from altitude sickness.

In the gaps of better weather, Wilson tried to make his way up the mountain to the North Col. He survived several nasty falls, but was defeated by an imposing 12m (40ft) wall of ice – daunting enough for an experienced climber, and impossible for a man who had previously only walked up a few steep hills.

Once again his diary recorded his triumphs and tribulations, such as when he stumbled across food and other equipment left by the 1933 expedition:

May 17: What do you think I had a couple of days ago? Anchovy paste from FORTNUM & MASON [an exclusive London food store]... There's enough equipment here to start a shop.

May 18: ... nothing of int. except that it snowed and blowed like the D. all day.

May 19: ... am as dirty as they make 'em. Fingernails black and dirt well ground into hands. Shall be glad when the show is over and I can become civilised again.

As the days passed, his handwriting deteriorated with his health and strength, and the dawning realization that he had set himself too great a task. Wilson was admired by his Sherpas – but their patience and faith in him was now exhausted. Deciding they would all be killed if they carried on, the Sherpas tried to persuade him to call off his climb. But having got this far, Wilson was not going to give up. He gave them instructions to wait for him for a fortnight and headed off alone, carrying his tent, some bread and oatmeal, a camera and a silk Union Jack. This had been signed by several female admirers, and he intended to plant it on the summit. The Sherpas called after him: "You go to your death!" But he waved cheerily, and pointed up at the top of the mountain.

On May 31, Wilson prepared for another attempt on the route to the North Col. Before he went, he made an optimistic entry in his journal: "Off again, gorgeous day." They were the last words he ever wrote.

❖

The Sherpas waited, and waited, and then they returned home. Maurice Wilson had vanished. A year passed with no further news. Then, in the spring of 1935, another British expedition arrived to climb the mountain. When the climbers reached the base of the North Col, 6,400m (21,000ft) up the mountain, they were surprised to see a pair of boots and the remains of a tent scattered before them. The scene took on a macabre aspect when one of the climbers, Charles Warren, saw the body of Maurice Wilson lying close by. Warren was soon joined by Eric Shipton, from the previous expedition, and another climber named Edwin Kempson.

The three men made a careful check of the scene, almost as a detective would in a murder investigation, and pieced together Wilson's final days. He had, they supposed, returned from another attempt up to the North Col. How successful he had been nobody knew, but at least he did not kill himself climbing. Instead, he had returned to his tent and died there, exhausted and defeated. During the winter a storm had blown the tent down, leaving both him and his possessions scattered around. His journal, rucksack, stove, even his silk Union Jack, were all found around him, but his sleeping bag had vanished.

All this established, there was only one thing left to do. Warren, Shipton and Kempson wrapped Maurice Wilson in his tent and carried him to a nearby crevasse. Here, they laid his body so it slipped down a steep incline into the deep, forbidding darkness below. Then they built a cairn of stones as a monument on the spot where his body was found. That night, the three climbers sat by the crevasse and read aloud from Wilson's journal. It was a sad, moving document, and each man found something to admire in Wilson's determined and courageous folly.

Strangely, even today, mountaineers pursuing the North Col route still stumble across Wilson's remains. They are occasionally disinterred by the constant motion of the slow-moving glacier, which has also broken up his body and clothing, spreading them over a wide area. His remains were last discovered by the 1999 expedition which set out to find Mallory and Irvine.*

"Occasionally, you find pieces of cloth in the glacier that look like they could have come from the 1930s," said expedition climber Jochen Hemmleb. "The first piece we found was half a femur bone about eight inches long. Not far from it I found one vertebra. Then about 600-900ft [180-270m] down from that was a piece of forearm… Even in death, he shows his determination, refusing to be buried…"

* See page 136.

The world intervenes

1935-1952

The British mounted three more expeditions to Everest in the 1930s, while other nations were refused permission to climb the mountain. The first of these expeditions, in 1935, marked the arrival of Sherpa Tenzing Norgay, then aged 20, who would go on to play a major role in the history of Everest. But further attempts in 1936 and 1938, all via the North Col route, made no further progress than those of the previous decade.

The Second World War broke out in 1939 and put a stop to Everest expeditions. Even after it ended in 1945, other events intervened to dash any immediate prospect of climbing the world's tallest mountain. India had always been the staging post for Everest expeditions, but in 1947 it gained its independence from the British empire. This brought with it other problems. In the north of the country the nation of Pakistan was created. Many of India's Muslims fled there, and in the process there was much bloodshed. Then Tibet, the country from which all Everest climbs had been made, declared it would temporarily close its borders to to foreigners. The upheaval caused by Indian independence had made an expedition inadvisable; this made one impossible. In 1950, China invaded and occupied Tibet, which effectively cut the country off from the rest of the world, ruling out this route to Everest for the foreseeable future. But, as so often happens, what seemed like a bad thing at the time turned out to have unforeseen advantages.

Tibet lies to the north of the Himalayas, but immediately south lies Nepal – in fact, the border between the two countries goes straight up and down the South East and West Ridges of Everest, crossing over the summit. Before the Chinese invasion of Tibet, Nepal had been a mysterious country, which had not allowed foreigners to visit. The invasion changed everything. All of a sudden Nepal needed friends, and Europeans and Americans found themselves welcome.

This was great news for climbers. Nepal, much of which is occupied by the Himalayas, contains some of the highest peaks in the world. For the first time ever, these were now available to climb. Access to Nepal also opened up another possibility with regard to Everest. Howard-Bury's 1922 expedition team had explored all of the territory surrounding Everest. They had sneaked into Nepal to check out the southern face of the mountain and had seen that the path to the lower slopes was blocked by fearsome obstacles. From 4,900m (16,000ft) to 6,100m (20,000ft) lay the Khumbu Glacier – a vast river of slow-moving ice, riddled with crevasses. Halfway down the glacier was a terrifying section of broken blocks called an icefall. Here, the ground beneath the ice dropped sharply, causing the glacier to break into a maze of gaping crevasses and huge chunks the size of tower blocks or cathedrals. Every now and then, one such massive slab would topple over, making a noise like the end of the world and crushing anything that lay beneath. Until the 1950s, that might have been an unwary crow or another one of the few animals that eked out an existence at 5,400m (18,000ft), but now it might be human beings. The icefall was, without doubt, the most dangerous place on the entire mountain.

Yet for anyone brave enough to risk a trip up the Khumbu Glacier, there were clear rewards. The glacier leads to a huge bowl of snow which climbers call the Western Cwm (*cwm* is a Welsh word for a hollow on a hillside). The Western Cwm has three huge peaks towering above it – Nuptse, Lhotse and Everest. From here, the route to the summit is plain to see. There is a steep ascent to the South Col – a flat, windblown plain between the two peaks of Lhotse and Everest. Then a steep seam of rock, called the South East Ridge, leads to the top of the mountain.

This new route was first explored in 1951 by a British expedition led by Eric Shipton. They intended to press up to the South Col, but Shipton was faced with a moral dilemma that no Everest expedition leader had previously had to consider.

The Khumbu icefall was obviously a dangerous route. A mountaineer who climbs for fun, and who has made a conscious decision to risk his life in pursuit of his hobby, can chose whether or not to take that risk. But the Sherpas made their living from helping climbers from other countries explore this mountain. Was it right to put their lives so deliberately at risk too? Shipton decided not. His expedition established that there was a possible route to the South Col, but they themselves did not go that far. The expedition did, however, offer a New Zealand climber named Edmund Hillary his first experience of the mountain. He would return a couple of years later, to try his luck again.

Through "Suicide Passage" with a handful of friends

The 1952 Swiss expedition

In the years after the Second World War, Britain's position in the world was changing. The British empire, which had covered one quarter of the world, was crumbling. Previously Britain had ruled over India and exercised a strong influence on surrounding countries, such as Tibet and Nepal, although they were not official British territories. This had enabled the Everest Committee to ensure that only British climbers got a crack at Everest. Requests from climbers of other nationalities, including Germans and Americans, were persistently denied.

But now, as Britain's influence declined, the Nepalese decided that a group of Swiss mountaineers should be given permission to try to climb the mountain in the spring and autumn of 1952. Switzerland, dominated as it was by the central European Alps, had produced many talented climbers. They had been applying for permission to climb Everest since 1926. Now their time had come. Two Swiss mountaineers, René Dittert and Edouard Wyss-Dunant had been planning this trip since 1949.

They put together what they described as "a handful of friends" – actually the cream of Swiss mountaineers, including Raymond Lambert, a climber of international fame.

British climbers were dismayed that the Swiss group had received permission, afraid that their rivals would succeed in reaching the summit on a first attempt while British groups had mounted seven failed expeditions. So they suggested a joint expedition and the Swiss mountaineers were interested, but the plan failed because no agreement could be reached as to which climbers should be included in the group. Still, despite the rivalry, Eric Shipton went to Switzerland to show the expedition photographs of the new route to the South Col.

There were several clear advantages in an approach through Nepal up to the South Col and beyond, rather than by the traditional North Col route. Very importantly, the most dangerous part of the climb, the Khumbu icefall, was at the start, when climbers were fresh and the altitude was not so crippling. On the North Col route, the two huge obstacles of the First and Second Steps guarded the final route to the summit – daunting hurdles for climbers near to exhaustion. Another advantage of the South Col route was that the way to the summit along the South East Ridge was broader, which meant there were more places to make camp. It also had firmer snow, was less windy, and was in sunshine for most of the day. Altogether, the South Col route now seemed a better, safer way to the top.

By now the Sherpas, who had started their careers as servants to the Europeans who hired them, had become experienced and very capable climbers in their own right. Increasingly, they began to be regarded as equals by the Europeans. Although the Sherpas still addressed European climbers as "Sahib", an Indian word meaning "Boss", times were changing. Recruited for this particular expedition was a 38-year-old Sherpa named Tenzing Norgay. Tenzing had been up Everest three times with British climbers before the war, and had risen to the rank of Sirdar – a Sherpa who hired and managed his own team of Sherpas. He was an excellent climber, and he seemed to share the Europeans' determination to reach the summit.

The Swiss established their Base Camp at Gorak Shep, near the Khumbu Glacier, on April 20, 1952. It took them until the middle of May to set up a series of camps across the glacier and get to the foot of the South Col. It was extremely hard work making their way across the glacier. In all the pinnacles and blocks of shaky ice, a climber could often see no more than a few feet in front of him. Taking the wrong route was exhausting, dispiriting, and happened all too frequently. One section of the icefall was so dangerous to go through, the climbers named it "Suicide Passage". But although there were several near misses, no one was killed or injured by falling ice or snow.

Eventually, the Swiss climbers and their Sherpas became the first people to stand in the Western Cwm, and a camp was set up there on May 6. They now had to figure out how to get up the steep slopes that led to the South Col. Of all possible routes, the most promising was up through a slab of black rock the climbers named the Geneva Spur. This way was not the most direct, but it provided the least chance of being swept away by an avalanche. The climb up was very difficult. At 7,300m (24,000ft), altitude had become a noticeable problem, and the mountaineers had to battle constantly against their own lethargy.

Writing about climbing up to the Col, René Dittert recalled resting halfway up a steep ice cliff while his climbing partner, whom he was roped to, took the lead: "I leaned my forehead on the axe and waited for my heart to calm down... I watched the rope running up between my legs. It rose slowly, by jerks of eight or twelve inches and I dreaded the moment when it would tighten again and I would have to start moving once more."

After a day's climbing, wrote Dittert, "our muscles were as if made of cotton, without elasticity or resilience. At five o'clock, with flabby legs and empty-headed, without feeling, we disappeared into our tents. Ten times I returned to the job of unstrapping my crampons and pulling off my boots."

During this section of the climb, a storm pinned the expedition down in the camp at the base of the Col slopes, causing them to scurry to their flimsy tents like frightened animals. Numbed by fierce cold for days on end, every climber wondered what on earth they were doing in such a dreadful place.

But the storm passed. By May 26, the Swiss were able to set up camp on the South Col and were ready for a summit attempt. Their plan was to make another camp on the South East Ridge above 8,380m (27,500ft). Here, two climbers could shelter overnight, then make a dash for the summit. This camp was set up the next day by four of the team. It was just a single tent, and the two climbers chosen to go for the top were Raymond Lambert and Tenzing Norgay. It was a telling moment in the shift from servants and guides to fellow adventurers when a Sherpa was chosen as one of the mountaineers to make an attempt on the summit.

Over the course of the trip, Lambert and Tenzing had become good friends, and they had developed a great respect for each other's abilities. Marvelling at Tenzing's strength and stamina at high altitude, Lambert had said, "Tenzing, you have got three lungs. The higher you go, the better you get." Tenzing, in turn, had a deep affection for Lambert, calling him, "My companion of the heights, and the closest and dearest of my friends."

They had no cooking equipment or sleeping bags. At that height, Lambert recalled, "Our legs would not obey us and our brains scarcely functioned." When night fell, it was so cold and their bodies became so stiff and numb, it felt as if they had been given an anaesthetic. The heavy-duty canvas duvet jackets the climbers wore offered some warmth when they were moving, but were not as effective while they lay still in their tents. Even without the cold, it was impossible to sleep – the wind roared like a jet plane, and avalanches rumbled in the distance like runaway trains. But this was a blessing. If the two had fallen asleep in such extreme cold, they would almost certainly never have woken up. As they waited for daylight, they had to beat each other's bodies to keep the circulation going and ward off frostbite, then huddle together to gain a little heat. Looking out of the tent and up to the night sky, Lambert recalled the stars were so unnaturally bright they filled him with fear. During the night they both developed a raging thirst, but had nothing to drink. A fragment of ice placed in an empty tin, and melted with a candle flame, was the best they could do.

Eventually the dawn came, and the two climbers emerged from their tent to stinging ice needles hurled by the wind onto their exposed faces. It was cloudy above and foggy below – not a good sign. But both Lambert and Tenzing felt they had come too far to give up. Lambert looked up at the ridge leading to the summit and winked. Tenzing nodded. Both men understood what they were going to do without even speaking.

It didn't take long to get ready. To keep warm during the night they had worn everything they now stood up in, apart from their crampons. After a numb struggle to place these on their boots they were off up to the top of the world.

But there were problems from the start. The high altitude sapped their strength. But worse still, the oxygen equipment they carried worked very poorly at that altitude. The Swiss had no qualms about using oxygen, but their sets repeatedly malfunctioned. Breathing through them required a great deal of effort – so much so that an exhausted climber couldn't climb and breathe at the same time. He had to climb and then stop to breathe oxygen.

Lambert and Tenzing struggled up the ridge, sometimes on all fours, at all times stopping for oxygen after every step. The weather grew worse, but finally the sun came out. As the mist burned away, they could see they were higher than the nearby peak of Lhotse (8,501m, or 27,890ft). But again the bad weather returned, and they were enveloped in fog and frozen snow. Lambert, especially, began to fear for his life. He felt exhausted, but elated – a sure sign of high-altitude sickness. He thought of Mallory and Irvine, and how they had vanished on the North Ridge, wondering if this was how they had felt just before they met with the mishap that ended their lives.

By now they had reached a spot about 200m (600ft) below the South Summit, but the wind was picking up, and the snow was stinging their faces. They had climbed just 200m (600ft) in five hours, and reached a new record height of 8,600m

(28,210ft). The summit lay only about 250m (800ft) above them. But they knew they couldn't possibly reach it. They were totally shattered. Once more, the decision to go back was made without a word. Both men knew they had been defeated by the mountain. It was time to return to the relative safety of the South Col. The Swiss team made another attempt the following day, but were halted by blizzards on the South Col. Still, they had shown just how much could be achieved on the new route.

The first Swiss route (1952)

Everest

Lhotse

Camp VII

Camp VI

Camp V

Camp IV

Camp III

Camp II

Camp I

The Swiss climbers returned, as planned, that autumn, almost certain that this time they would succeed. But their second expedition was less successful. Although they managed to establish a camp on the South Col, the weather was atrocious, climbers were struck by ill health, and a Sherpa was killed by falling shards of ice – the first man to die on Everest since Maurice Wilson in 1934. The Swiss mountaineers had tried their hardest, but the summit remained unconquered. The next year a British-led expedition was due to try the new route. Could they succeed where every other team had failed?

The world beneath their boots

The 1953 British expedition

The near success of the Swiss team in 1952 had badly rattled the Himalayan Committee, as the Everest Committee had recently been renamed. As they prepared for their own attempt in 1953, the pressure to succeed was intense. The new South Col route offered such promising possibilities that the summit seemed to be there for the taking. Whoever mounted the next attempt would have, the Committee felt, no real excuse to fail.

There was another reason, too, for wanting a British expedition to succeed in reaching the top that year. Britain's wartime monarch, King George VI, had died in 1952, and his daughter, Princess Elizabeth, was due to be crowned in June 1953. The years immediately after the Second World War had been dreary ones in Britain, and now there was talk of a "new Elizabethan era" of prosperity and progress. What better way to mark the coronation and the start of this new period of history than by having a British climbing team conquer the world's most notorious mountain?

The first thing to decide was who would be the

leader. What the 1953 expedition needed, the Himalayan Committee felt, was a good organizer. And they knew just the man for the job. His name was Colonel John Hunt. He was 43 years old and was an undisputed genius at arranging transportation and supplies. Hunt was also a distinguished climber, though not terribly well known.

Hunt took up his job in October 1952 and, right from the start, there was a strong military style to his leadership. This was nothing new – many of the climbers considered to have "the right stuff" by the Everest and Himalayan Committees were military men. Their jobs, after all, required them to be fit, to be "team players" who could get along with other people in difficult circumstances, and to have personal qualities such as drive, discipline, determination and courage – all the character traits that best suited expedition mountaineers. Also, the armed forces were always happy to allow men leave for such activities, unlike many of the employers of other non-military climbers, who were civil servants, doctors, lecturers and the like. (Perhaps it was the influence of military men on climbing expeditions that led to mountaineering being described in warlike terms. Everest was to be "conquered" by an "assault team", and getting to the top would be a "victory" for Britain, failing would be a "defeat".)

Hunt planned the trip down to the last detail, and was allowed to spare no expense when it came to acquiring the best equipment. In fact, much of the equipment came cheap or free from manufacturers anxious to lend their names to such a potentially prestigious enterprise. There was to be no dithering about oxygen, either. Unsporting or not, its advantages were obvious, and Hunt's climbers were going to use it.

The team he chose, along with the veteran mountaineer Eric Shipton, looked very promising. There were ten experienced and capable climbers, among them Charles Evans, Tom Bourdillon, Alfred Gregory and a couple of New Zealanders, George Lowe and Edmund Hillary, who had been with Shipton on his 1951 expedition. Strictly speaking, of course, the New Zealanders weren't exactly "British", but in those days the ties between Britain and the Commonwealth countries were especially close, and both men had roots that could be traced back to Britain. Hillary's family, for example, came from Yorkshire stock, and he had a brusque "speak-as-I-find" manner that would not have been out of place in the county of his ancestors. He was good-natured, immensely tall, and bristled with restless energy.

Extra team members were kept to a minimum. Physiologist Griff Pugh came to study how the team adapted to high altitudes, and cameraman Tom Stobart and *Times* journalist James Morris came along to cover the story. In exchange for sponsorship, Morris had been given exclusive access to the expedition, although other newspapers also sent journalists out to Nepal to sniff out as much as they could about this fascinating story.

❖

The expedition met in Kathmandu, the capital of Nepal, in early March. Here the climbers met the expedition Sherpas, gathered together by Tenzing Norgay, who had climbed so successfully with Raymond Lambert the previous year. Things got off to a bad start. While the expedition climbers were offered accommodation in the British Embassy, the Sherpas were put up in an Embassy garage, which didn't even have a lavatory. They all protested the next morning by urinating in the street outside the garage, an act which caused outrage among Embassy staff and great interest among Western journalists.

During this era, relations between the Sherpas and the climbers were changing. The Swiss, especially, had treated their Sherpas as equals, although it was still understood that their principal role was to carry equipment. The British, however, had dominated the Indian subcontinent for three centuries, and had not quite shaken off the notion that their Sherpas were servants belonging to an inferior racial group.

The trek to Everest's South side was a more difficult one than the pre-war route through Tibet had been. Tibet was flat enough for pack animals, and a climber and his gear could be transported on the back of a yak or pony. The route through Nepal, however, was too bumpy for animals, so everyone had to walk. This was hard work, but it helped to build fitness and stamina, and ensure a climber was in top condition by the time he arrived at Everest. The route was also very beautiful, especially compared to the dreary, dusty plains of Tibet.

Throughout April, the expedition worked its way up the Khumbu Glacier and through the treacherous icefall. Hunt's team found this route just as unpleasant as the Swiss had done. The names they gave particularly dangerous spots – Hellfire Alley, Hillary's Horror, Atom-bomb Area – show them trying to make light of their anxieties. By early May they had reached the Western Cwm.

It was noticeable right from the start that Hillary and Tenzing hit it off spectacularly well. Both men seemed to like each other and, more importantly, they climbed wonderfully together. Each recognized the ability of the other, and a competitive bond seemed to develop between them – they wanted to surpass each other in daring and perseverance, and also, as a duo, outdo the rest of the team.

Of Hillary, Tenzing said: "he was a wonderful climber... and had great strength and endurance. Like many men of action, and especially the British, he did not talk much, but he was nevertheless a fine cheerful companion; and he was popular with the Sherpas, because in things like food and equipment he always shared whatever he had."

Hillary spoke well of Tenzing, too: "[He] really

looked the part – larger than most Sherpas, he was very strong and active; his flashing smile was irresistible; and he was incredibly patient and obliging…" Hillary also spoke of his transparent, almost ruthless determination, and said of them both: "We wanted for the expedition to succeed – and nobody worked harder to ensure that it did."

❖

On May 7, Hunt called the climbers together to announce his plans for the assault on the summit. There would be compulsory use of oxygen above Camp V, which had been set up on the edge of the Western Cwm. After all, what was the point of a climber wearing himself out on the lower slopes, when he needed all his reserves of energy for the top of the mountain?

There would be a two-pronged assault on the summit. First to go for the top, said Hunt, would be Charles Evans and Tom Bourdillon. They would open up the route to the South Summit, a hump of rock and snow just 100m (300ft) lower than the real summit, then head for the top if they could. Going with them some of the way, Hunt, Gregory and five Sherpas would carry any necessary equipment, such as oxygen, and a tent. The next day Hillary and Tenzing, also accompanied for part of the way by other climbers and Sherpas, would go up the ridge and make a camp around 8,500m (28,000ft). The idea was that they would spend the night there, and then head for the summit on the next day. Hunt's plan was a clever one, because it spread the burden of carrying supplies, saving the strength of the men designated to reach the summit for the final push to the top.

The first step was to reach the South Col, the dip between Lhotse and Everest where the South East Ridge began. While the climbers were trying to reach the Col, the weather turned intensely cold and windy, and it was not until May 22 that Camp VIII was established there. The expedition followed a route which took them up the Lhotse Glacier and then down a few hundred feet on to the Col. Hunt called the Col: "as dreary and desolate place as I ever expect to see… It was a queer sensation to go down like this at the end of our long, hard climb, as though entering a trap; and this feeling was heightened by the scene which we were approaching. For there before us were the skeletons of the Swiss tents… they stood, just the bare metal poles supported still by their frail guy ropes, all but a few shreds of the canvas ripped from them by the wind."

❖

May 26 was designated "summit day". Hunt and two Sherpas set off up the South East Ridge, carrying equipment for Camp IX, and Bourdillon and Evans followed an hour later. They were having problems with their oxygen equipment, but once it was sorted out, they soon overtook the earlier party.

While their equipment was working properly, Bourdillon and Evans made great progress. They reached the foot of the South Summit by one o'clock that afternoon. They were at a record 8,750m (28,700ft) – higher than anyone had ever stood before. But although the summit was within reach, Evans' oxygen gear was causing problems again. He could hardly breathe and was dangerously exhausted. The two climbers had been determined to reach the top of the mountain, but they did not want to lose their lives in the attempt. The climb ahead was still difficult, and the return would be even more perilous. Downcast, they turned back to the South Col, having worn themselves to the point of death.

Hillary, who was up at the South Col camp, watched them return: "They moved silently towards us – a few stiff, jerky paces – then stop. Then a few more paces. They were very near complete exhaustion… From head to foot they were encased with ice. There was ice on their clothing, on their oxygen sets and on their rope. It was hanging from their hair and beards and eyebrows; they must have had the most terrible time in the wind and snow."

Lesser men would have looked at Bourdillon and Evans, and feared to follow in their footsteps. But Hillary was different. Whatever fears he had, he kept them to himself. As a child he had devoured adventure books by Edgar Rice Burroughs, Rider Haggard and John Buchan. His greatest fantasy was to be a hero, and now, as an adult, fate was offering him an unrepeatable opportunity.

❖

Hunt's plan required Hillary and Tenzing to try for the top the following day, but it was too windy. May 28 seemed more promising. So began the expedition's last chance to succeed. According to plan, Lowe and Gregory and a Sherpa named Ang Nyima set off from the South Col first, carrying food supplies and equipment for Hillary and Tenzing, who followed soon after. At 8,500m (28,000ft) Lowe's party dropped off their gear and left Hillary and Tenzing to put up a tent. It was half past two in the afternoon, and both men found the task of finding a suitable spot to put up the tent completely draining. In the end they found a sloping spot that had to be flattened, but this still left one half higher than the other. Tenzing placed his sleeping bag on the lower section, right next to an alarming drop.

Hunt's strategy of spreading the hauling of equipment so the summit teams would have the best possible chance of getting to the top was paying off. After putting up the tent, Hillary and Tenzing still had sufficient energy to spend the rest of the afternoon drinking large quantities of hot lemon, and they even managed a meal. Lowe's team had brought up enough cylinders for them to be able to breathe oxygen during the night, as well as on their trek up the mountain. Bodies starved of oxygen are far more susceptible to cold, so having the gas to breathe in the tent kept them warmer and helped them to sleep.

After the best sleep anyone camping at 8,500m (28,000ft) could possibly hope to have, they fuelled up on more hot lemon and set off up to the summit at half past six on the morning of May 29. Climbing conditions were poor and they needed every ounce of their strength. A crust of thin ice had formed on the snow, and with every step they sank up to their knees. Presently they reached the South Summit, the spot where Evans and Bourdillon had decided it would be fatal to carry on. Bourdillon had considered going around a particularly dangerous-looking snow slope, but Hillary knew their best chance lay in a speedy ascent, even if it meant taking huge risks. For Tenzing, it was the most dangerous place he had ever been on a mountain. The thought of climbing that slope would haunt him for years to come.

Hillary seized the moment, telling himself: "This is Everest and you've got to take a few risks." It was a phrase he repeated often to himself on that day. Edging warily up the slope, his stomach tight with fear, he expected the snow to avalanche at any moment, sweeping both him and Tenzing to their deaths. But the loose snow held in place, and once Hillary had attached a firm rope, Tenzing scurried up after him. By nine o'clock that morning they were at the top of the South Summit, and higher than anyone else had ever been on the mountain. They looked up to the summit itself, still a few hundred feet above them. The path up there was a series of enormous cornices – mounds of snow blown by the wind into solid ledges overhanging the edge of the mountain.

Mountaineers had guessed that the South East Ridge would offer an easier route to the top, but there were still sections where a man could lose his life in an instant. The snow slope had been a terrifying ordeal, but there was worse to come. As they trudged up the ridge they were confronted by a thin, vertical slab of rock and ice about 12m (40ft) high. On one side, the South West Face plunged sharply away, on the other side, the Kangshung Face ran steeply down – both offered a fast and fatal trip down the mountain.

But both men instinctively felt this was their final hurdle. Once up here, the way to the top was theirs. Hillary noticed that there was a small, funnel-like hollow between the rock on one side and ice on the other. He would have to press his back against the ice and lever himself up, with his crampon boots on the ice. The drawback of this particular technique was that if the ice gave way, then he would go flying off down the Kangshung Face to certain death.

Hillary pushed gingerly with a boot against the ice. It held firm. Then, taking his life into his hands, he held onto the rock and braced his back against the ice, digging his boots in under him, so that the whole "chimney" took his full weight. It held. Slowly, he levered himself upwards, expecting at any second the cracking sound of splintering ice that would herald his death. But still the ice held firm. After a half-hour struggle, he wriggled his way to the top and lay there, in his own words, "gasping like a fish". When he had recovered, Tenzing followed him up. For every future Everest mountaineer, this treacherous guardian of the summit would be known as the Hillary Step.

They carried on up the sloping ridge, taking care not to wander too close to the overhanging cornice. Then, at the top of one slope, they noticed the only way further on was down. They had reached the summit! It was half past eleven in the morning and, far below, they could see the East Rongbuk Glacier and the high plateau of Tibet. The view was God-like in its scope and magnificence – Hillary would later write: "I had the world lie beneath my clumsy boots." Both men were grinning wildly. Hillary offered Tenzing a rather formal handshake, but Tenzing returned his gesture with a huge hug. They had achieved the impossible, but their feeling of triumph was tempered by the knowledge that they still faced a very dangerous return journey.

Hillary stared down at the North Ridge and thought of Mallory and Irvine. He looked around him for any clue that they had reached the summit but, if they had, nearly three decades of snowstorms and gales had obliterated the evidence. Then he buried a crucifix John Hunt had given him, and

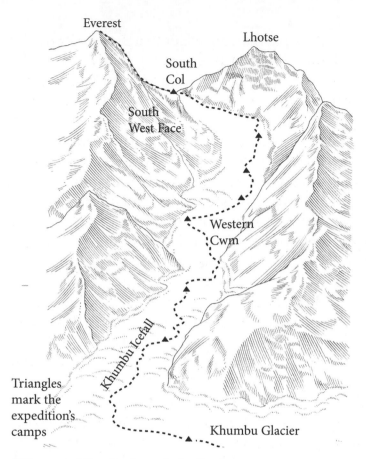

Hillary and Tenzing's route to the top

Tenzing too buried some offerings to his Buddhist gods.

As Tenzing unfurled a series of flags on his ice-axe (they had brought the flags of the United Nations, Great Britain, Nepal and India), Hillary busied himself taking photographs. There were to be no photographs of Hillary – as he later explained rather brusquely, "Tenzing is no photographer, and Everest was no place to begin teaching him."

There was time for a brief snack, so the two men sat together on the summit, higher than anyone else in the world, and shared a slice of Kendal Mint Cake – a piece of mountaineering history and product endorsement that millions of pounds worth of advertising could never hope to buy. (The "cake" isn't really cake at all, but a very sweet, minty fudge, which climbers eat to give themselves an energy boost.) Then it was time to return.

On the way down they passed some half-empty oxygen cylinders, discarded by Evans and Bourdillon, which they still had enough strength to carry down the mountain. Then, eventually, the South Col camp came into view. Hillary's friend, George Lowe, and a Sherpa had been waiting for them. Hillary, in his brisk New Zealand way, and with no appreciation of how the momentous news would be reported in future accounts, announced their triumph by shouting, "Well George, we knocked the b****** off!"

They had done it, and they were still alive.

❖

Down at Camp IV, Hunt and the rest of his team waited in a state of high anticipation. The expedition had been equipped with radios. But due to a quirk in the landscape, they worked only intermittently in the Western Cwm. Lowe had been instructed to send a signal down from his camp, but it was too foggy. For Hunt, the strain had been extraordinary. Photographs from the trip show him peering into the camera like a wizened 60 year old, yet he was only in his mid-40s. He had worked tirelessly to ensure the success of this attempt, and now he was about to learn whether his efforts had paid off.

Eventually, the climbers returned from the South Col. At first, those waiting at Camp IV could just see four distant specks. That was good news in itself – at least no one had been killed in the summit attempt. Then, as the climbers got nearer, the men at the camp searched for gestures or any other indication that would suggest a victory or defeat. But cameraman Tom Stobart had planned this moment, and was stage-managing it for his film. He dashed on ahead and asked the four not to give anything away until they were almost back at the camp. Then he returned and began filming their arrival. As Hillary and Tenzing grew nearer, Hunt and his men rushed towards them. Only then did they raise their arms in triumph, and the whole party erupted in celebration – all neatly framed for the film.

James Morris knew he had the hottest news story in the world. He also wanted it to break in time for the Queen's coronation. He talked to Hillary and Tenzing, then despatched a runner to the Indian radio post at Namche Bazar. He carried a coded message which read: "Summit of Everest reached on 29 May by Hillary and Tenzing". From here, it was transmitted to the British Embassy in Kathmandu, and from there to London and *The Times*.

News broke in Britain on June 2, the very morning of the coronation. *The Times*, of course, had the full story, with other papers rewriting what was reported in it. This item from *The News Chronicle* gives a taste of the mixture of national pride and elation brought on by the news:

THE CROWNING GLORY:
EVEREST IS CLIMBED

Tremendous news for the Queen
Hillary does it

Glorious Coronation Day news! Everest –
Everest the unconquerable – has been
conquered... The news came late last night
that Edmund Hillary and the Sherpa guide
Tenzing, of Colonel Hunt's expedition,
had climbed to the summit of Earth's
highest peak...

The significance of the event was appreciated world-wide. *The New York Times* declared: "man has completed his conquest of the world", and went on to say, "Hillary... and Tenzing... will take their place with Sir Walter Raleigh and Sir Francis Drake."

One major controversy remained. Who had got there first? Both men refused to answer. "We got there together", or "We got there at almost the same time", they would snap rather peevishly. Eventually, Tenzing spilled the beans in his biography, *Tiger of the Snows*. It was Hillary. But, as Hillary pointed out in his own account: "We shared the work, the risks, and the success – it was a team effort and nothing else is important."

"Someday Everest will be climbed again"

After the 1953 Expedition

When Hillary and Tenzing reached the top, there was a general feeling that Everest had been "done". Now this most difficult of mountains had finally been conquered, many thought that would be the end of the story. John Hunt, leader of the 1953 expedition, noted in his account of the climb (published a mere six months later): "Someday Everest will be climbed again", but he assumed that for the time being at least, climbers would lose interest in this great mountain. But such is the attraction of the highest spot on Earth that, fifty years after men first reached the summit, Everest is still a source of novelty and news. A search for "Mount Everest" on the Internet, for example, reveals more than 116,000 websites.

The 1953 triumph was not the end. Hillary and Tenzing might have reached the summit first, but there was still the challenge of taking a different route. Later climbers have done just that. In 1960, a Chinese expedition scaled the North Col and reached the top via the North and North East Ridges, successfully completing what Mallory, Shipton, Smythe and all the other pre-war pioneers had failed to do. In 1963, an American team went up the West Ridge and down the South East Ridge, the first successful traverse of the mountain. In 1975, a British team climbed the South West Face. This was also the year when the first woman, Junko Tabei of Japan, reached the summit. Altogether there are roughly 15 major routes to the top and, as each of these has been climbed, so mountaineers have sought different ways of claiming a "first".

The odd couple

Messner and Habeler's 1978 attempt

As climbers sought new ways to claim a "first" on Everest, it was inevitable that the "oxygen debate", so hotly disputed in the 1920s and 30s, would make a comeback. Hunt's 1953 expedition had settled once and for all the effectiveness of oxygen, and for the next 25 years, it was accepted that to get to the summit, a climber had to use oxygen. But during the mid-1970s a couple of exceptional Alpine climbers decided to champion the cause of "natural" mountaineering, and try for the summit without.

Italian Reinhold Messner and Austrian Peter Habeler were climbing's odd couple. In the words of Everest historian Walt Unsworth, they looked like "every schoolgirl's ideal ski instructor". Lithe, handsome and charming, they had an almost telepathic link, which enabled them to climb together with formidable speed and daring. But for all their brilliance as a team, there was no particular friendship between them. Peter Habeler explained the differences thus: "The applause of the general public is not as important to me. But Reinhold needs recognition. He likes to appear on television; he needs the interviews in the newspapers. His birth sign is Virgo, he likes to shine, where as I am a Cancerian who crawls back into his shell. I don't like any heroic poses."

Both believed passionately that climbing should be as simple as possible. Messner even shunned the common technique of driving metal protection pegs into a rock face to hold a climber if he should fall. The results were an astonishing increase in speed, coupled with a much greater risk of death. Messner's daring was all the more extraordinary considering his brother had been killed on a climb they had made together on the Himalayan mountain of Nanga Parbat.

Messner was "New Age" before the term was invented. One of his books, *The Crystal Horizon*, describes mountaineering as "a symbol of the outermost frontier of the world and the innermost frontier of the ego". With regard to oxygen, he once said, "Mountains are so elemental that humans do not have the right to subdue them with technology."

❖

Having reached the decision to try for the top without oxygen, Messner and Habeler were immediately grounded by bureaucracy. The Nepalese government had a backlog of requests to climb Everest, so the two climbers asked to join an Austrian expedition already cleared for an attempt in the spring of 1978. The leader of this expedition, Wolfgang Nairz, was pleased to have a couple of climbers with such great expertise join his team, and generously made space for them. The aims of his expedition were many – aside from making a first Austrian attempt on the summit, there were plans to try a new route up the South Spur, and even hang-glide down from the South Col. Now they would also include an attempt on the summit without oxygen.

The expedition approached Everest via the Western Cwm, and Base Camp was set up before the Khumbu Glacier in late March. Messner and Habeler were climbing so well, Nairz made their oxygen-free assault his first priority. All set to go for the top by April 23, the pair then hit a major hurdle. Peter Habeler ate a can of sardines which gave him food poisoning. On the way up to the South Col, he became so ill with sickness and stomach cramps he could not continue climbing, and he was forced to return to Base Camp.

Messner, supremely fit and full of confidence, decided to go on alone. He and two Sherpas, named Mingma and Ang Dorje, set up camp on the South Col that night. But they completed their journey to the Col in a terrible storm, and struggled in a fierce gale to set up a tent. The blizzard was so bad, Messner wondered if their tent would be ripped to pieces or if they would be blown off the Col. There was nothing to do but stay under cover and wait for the weather to improve. This was a fine plan for the short term, but the storm continued relentlessly. Sleep in such a cauldron of noise and cold was impossible. Then, as Messner had feared, the tent ripped open. Mingma was so cold and exhausted he could not be roused from his sleeping bag, but Messner and Ang Dorje knew that if they didn't set up another tent, they would die. The two men struggled for an hour in the teeth of the wind and the stinging, icy snow, trying to erect a new tent. Eventually they succeeded, and all three crawled in. Messner was so drained he burst into tears.

The whole of the next day, the storm raged outside. If this tent ripped open too, the three men would certainly die. Mingma and Ang Dorje had quietly decided their lives were over, and accepted their fate quite calmly. Messner, too, was slowly dying of cold and altitude sickness, but he was determined that they were all going to survive. He harangued his listless companions, forcing them to eat and drink.

Fortunately, on the morning of their third day on the Col, the storm lifted, and Messner and the Sherpas returned as quickly as they could to the Western Cwm. From there, Messner returned to Base Camp to rejoin Habeler. On the route back, he nearly died when a ladder taking him over a particularly difficult section of the icefall collapsed beneath him.

The next few days brought perfect weather and the rest of the expedition pressed ahead. Over the next week Wolfgang Nairz and three other climbers reached the summit.

The approach via
the South Col

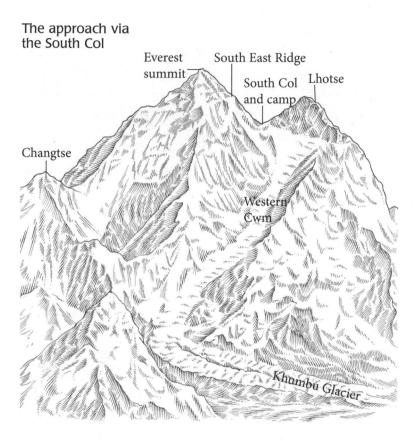

Changtse

Everest summit

South East Ridge

South Col and camp

Lhotse

Western Cwm

Khumbu Glacier

Meanwhile, back at Base Camp, Messner and Habeler were regaining their strength. Habeler had lost confidence in the idea of an assault without oxygen. But after several acrimonious arguments, the pair set out again for the South Col on May 7. With them were an English cameraman, Eric Jones, and three Sherpas. They were determined not to use oxygen, but brought a couple of cylinders with them in case of an emergency.

After a night on the Col, Messner and Habeler set off up the South East Ridge at half past five in the morning. They carried only the lightest of loads. Nairz's team had set up a camp on the ridge, which they could use if they needed. Conditions on the ridge were not good. A storm was raging and there was soft snow underfoot, which took much effort to wade through. Habeler described his state of mind at the time: "I saw only my feet, the next steps and handholds. I was moving automatically... The air became thinner and thinner, and I was near to suffocation. I still remember that a single word went through my mind, matching the rhythm of my steps: 'Forward, Forward, Forward.'"

Eventually the two climbers reached the South Summit, pressed on until they were above the storm clouds, and emerged into a clear blue sky. The sunshine gave them extra strength to keep moving up, but Habeler was half-disappointed that the weather was improving. He was so tired he was looking for an excuse to call off the climb.

The Hillary Step loomed before them. Both men made this hair-raising ascent with ice and snow breaking away from their footholds and tumbling down the dizzying drops on either side. They reached the top of the Step, but this dangerous section had done them both in. They lay face down in the snow, gasping for breath in the thin air. Eventually they felt the strength returning to their legs, and pressed on to the summit. The last section up to the top was an easy climb, but Habeler noted: "I was physically finished. I seemed to step outside myself and had the illusion that another person was walking in my place."

They reached the summit at around one o'clock that afternoon. It was an emotional moment. Not given to sharing confidences, or even socializing together, the two men hugged and wept with relief and joy, the tears freezing on their beards. But Habeler, especially worried about high-altitude sickness, was anxious to return down the mountain as soon as possible. Messner, though, remained on the summit to enjoy his triumph. Alone at the top, he unpacked a film cassette for his small movie camera. He was so befuddled he threw the tape away rather than the packaging it was wrapped in. He was, in this most isolated spot, "a single narrow gasping lung, floating over the mists and the summits".

❖

Habeler hurried down the mountain, feeling too tired for words. Once he had achieved his goal, he wanted to get back to safety as quickly as possible. Sometimes he crawled on all fours, sometimes he stumbled one step at a time. Then he began to see double – an especially hazardous condition when one wrong step can mean a fall of thousands of feet.

Somewhere down the ridge, he slipped, sat down with a jarring bump, and began to slide down the mountain. Habeler was so tired now, he was hardly conscious of his own actions. Automatically he plunged his ice-axe into the ground, and came to an arm-wrenching halt. He found himself in a sloping field of fresh snow, which could avalanche at any second. With great care, he picked his way slowly back onto firm ground and, eventually, he saw the South Col camp below.

A final slope lay between him and Eric Jones, three Sherpas and survival. Elated, Habeler jumped onto the slope to slide down it, and the snow immediately began to avalanche. Eric Jones, watching from the Col, was convinced Habeler was doomed. Caught in the cascade, he slid down in a mad flurry of white mist, but eventually slowed to a halt just as he reached the Col. He had gained a twisted ankle and lost his ice-axe and snow goggles, but at least he was alive. Jones ran towards him, to find Habeler mumbling incoherently, tears streaming down his face. But, brushes with death notwithstanding, Habeler had made it from the summit to the South Col in one extraordinary hour – a speedy descent unimaginable to previous climbers.

❖

Messner arrived an hour and a half later. He was in a bad way, suffering from snow blindness. During the climb he had frequently removed his snow goggles to use his video camera, and now he was suffering the consequences.

The climbers were too exhausted to return to the Western Cwm and had to spend another night in the "death zone". It was a nightmare. On top of their other troubles, another blizzard blew up, and cold gnawed at their burned-out bodies. Messner's eyes were causing him agony, too – but even this was not quite the emergency he had had in mind when the climbers had carried their two oxygen cylinders up to the camp. He refused to take any oxygen, even though it would have warmed him up and helped to ease his pain.

Next day, the storm was still raging. The climbers were in a bad way. Aside from their exhaustion, Messner could barely see, Habeler had a twisted ankle, and Jones was beginning to suffer from frostbite. But they all knew they had to return to the Cwm that morning, or die on the mountain. Their luck held. They met two of Nairz's climbers, who were on their way to another summit assault. One of them was a doctor, and he carried out vital first aid on Messner's eyes. Eventually they reached the Advanced Base Camp on the Cwm. Only then did they know for certain that they had escaped with their lives.

"As heavy as a corpse"

Reinhold Messner's 1980 solo attempt

Being the first to climb to the summit without oxygen was not enough of a challenge for Reinhold Messner. Now he planned a feat of even greater daring: a solo climb. Several climbers had reached the top on their own, but they had been with companions until the very last section, and had been part of large expeditions. Messner wanted to do the whole climb alone and without oxygen – with no back-up, no Sherpas and no additional supplies – just the equipment he carried himself. It was a crazy idea, but if anyone had the courage and guts to carry it off, it was him.

Such is the popularity of Everest, mountaineers have to apply for permission to climb it at least a couple of years in advance of their actual expedition. They go to the Nepalese or Chinese government (depending on which way they want to approach the mountain) and pay a fee, the size of which varies according to the number of climbers in the expedition. Messner realized it would be difficult for him to get permission for a solo climb, not least because it would earn the Nepalese or Chinese government so little money. So he deliberately booked his climb away from the most popular times, in the spring or at the end of the summer, when the weather was at its least dangerous. Instead, he asked if he could go during the Monsoon. The Chinese agreed, and charged him $50,000. They also insisted he took an interpreter, a liaison officer and a doctor. Messner had to put up with the first two of these unwanted companions, but he managed to convince the Chinese authorities to let him take his girlfriend, Nena Holguin, as the team doctor (although her only medical qualification was a first-aid certificate).

The plan was to go up the North Face, via Tibet, taking the same route as Mallory and Irvine from the North Col and up the North Ridge. But when Messner's tiny party arrived at the mountain, they found the snow was too soft and deep for safe climbing. The party retreated and spent a couple of weeks exploring other mountains. Then they returned for another look. This time the snow had hardened, and conditions were just right. There was also a break forecast in the Monsoon. This was exactly the opportunity Messner had hoped for.

❖

On August 16, he and Nena Holguin set up their Base Camp at the foot of the Col. On August 17, Messner shot up the slopes to a crevasse that lay at the edge of the Col. Here, he left a 20kg (44lb) rucksack containing the equipment he thought he would need – no more than a small tent, sleeping bag, plastic mattress, ice-axe and crampons, stove and a small supply of food. Then he went to bed early. On August 18, at five o'clock in the morning, he set off. He was up to the spot where he had left his rucksack in an amazing hour and a half. The dawn was barely breaking as the North Col lay before him. Then, he did something even a novice could usually manage to avoid – he fell into the crevasse.

After falling for what he described as "an eternity in slow motion", Messner came to a bone-jarring halt 8m (25ft) below. He was lucky nothing was broken. Fortunately, he had landed on a snow platform. He didn't know how thin the snow supporting him might be, and was terribly aware that it could give way at any second, leaving him to plunge to the bottom of the crevasse with no hope of rescue. All around him it was pitch black, apart from a small hole above, where he could see a single twinkling star.

The fall had taken away his will to continue climbing. "If I can climb out of here, I'm going straight back down this crevasse-ridden snowfield and we're packing up and heading home," he told himself. He thought of his girlfriend tucked up in her warm sleeping bag, and wondered if she could get a rope to him to save him. But then he realized she had no idea where he was, and there was no hope that anyone else might find him either. If he was to get out of this crevasse alive, it would be up to him.

Messner took stock of his situation. There was nothing else to do but edge up the narrow ledge which led to the top of the crevasse. His luck held, and soon he was out in the open air again. Having escaped with his life, Messner was now taunted by doubts. This, surely, was an omen. He should return to camp, and forget about the whole stupid idea. But on the other hand, if he could survive a fall into a crevasse, then he could cope with anything. He headed out over the North Col and, as he reached the North Ridge, the sun rose. Bit by bit, the mountain was gradually bathed in a magnificent honey-gold glow. It was turning out to be a beautiful day. Messner's optimism returned and he pressed on, establishing a smooth rhythm to his steps, and feeling very much at one with this world of rock and snow.

The whole day he trudged through thick snow, then made camp on a small platform half-way up the Ridge at 7,800m (25,600ft). Here, he was bothered by the feeling that he was no longer alone, but had an invisible companion sitting beside him. This is a common phenomenon on Everest with climbers who are on their own, especially if they are very tired or under great stress. Some people find their invisible partner an irritating presence, but others find it comforting. Messner, who saw climbing as a spiritual experience, decided he would welcome his friend. He was in good spirits as he set up his tent. The sun warmed his body and he felt full of confidence as he munched a meal of dried meat and had some salty Tibetan tea. As the daylight faded, leaving stark, black shadows on the landscape below, the sky turned from blue to orange, and then to red. That night his sleep was disturbed by the occasional rush of wind, but he woke the next morning feeling well prepared for the ordeal to come.

❖

Messner made a later start, setting off after nine o'clock in the morning, when the sun began to shine on the mountain. The climbing conditions were no better than the previous day, with thick snow which was very tiring to wade through. Messner told himself he would never get anywhere this way, and made an astonishingly brave decision. The route he had planned to take had been climbed before, but as it was such hard-going, he would try another route – up across the North Face and on to the Great Couloir, a huge gully that ran up to the summit pyramid. No one had ever been this way before.

The new route was highly dangerous, not least because snow from above could easily cascade down. But as Messner observed this great swathe of rock and snow, he noticed that several avalanches had recently swept across the Face, and he decided that there was unlikely to be another one just yet.

Crossing the North Face was slow, hard work, which filled him with anxiety. Anything – snow, rocks, ice, even a freak gust of wind – could sweep him off his feet and leave him tumbling to his death. As he climbed, his thoughts turned to Mallory and Irvine, the legendary climbers whose courage, daring and mysterious fate still intrigued mountaineers the world over. During a brief rest, Messner even imagined he could hear the long-dead British climbers calling to each other, their final, weary cries forever carried by the wind around the upper reaches of the mountain.

He carried on up, ten paces forward, then a rest to regain his breath. Occasionally Messner found himself fighting back a panicky feeling that he had gone too far to return safely. Mist descended around him, blotting out the warmth of the sun. But Messner was concentrating so hard on climbing and fighting his mounting exhaustion that he didn't really notice how dangerous the weather was becoming.

When the light began to fade and evening came, he was disappointed by how little progress he had managed to make. Most of the day had been spent moving across the mountain, rather than going up it. He had reached 8,200m (26,900ft) – a mere 400m (1,300ft) higher than he had been the day before.

Messner set up camp on a little ridge overlooking a plunging drop. He was within reach of the summit, but the longer he stayed at that altitude, the weaker he would become. That night he had to force himself to eat, drinking down large quantities of luke-warm soup and tea. Then he found it difficult to sleep. He could feel the strength and determination ebbing out of his body, and he wondered how he would find his way back to his tent if the mist grew thicker. The high altitude had dried his throat so much, he felt his windpipe was made of wood.

❖

Daybreak brought bad news. Although the summit above was bathed in a red glow, clouds were already gathering around the mountain and snow was beginning to fall. It was now or never. Besides, Messner realized, tomorrow he could be too weak to try for the top. He left everything he could at his tiny camp, taking only his crampons, ice-axe and camera. He picked his way through the Great Couloir and then onto the rocky North Pillar. Because of the falling snow, he could barely see more than 50m (150ft) in front of him, but he kept heading up.

The higher he got, the more difficult it was to breathe. Now he could go no more than 10 paces at a time before he had to stop to get his breath back. He talked to his ice-axe as if it were an old friend, and again he imagined he could hear voices in the wind. The climb seemed to go on forever, and Messner slowed to a crawl. He could manage only one or two paces before he had to stop, gasping down huge lungfuls of thin air. Acutely aware that a slip here would be fatal, he had to concentrate hard with every step, which wore him out even more. At times, he crept forward on all fours. His heavy boots, he remembered, felt "like anchors in the snow".

Messner carried on like this for another three hours, climbing almost in a trance, continually driving himself on. Even when he stopped to breathe, each breath burned his throat. But just as he felt he could go no further, he saw a cluster of discarded equipment and ribbons above him – it was the summit. The realization that he was nearly at the top brought no extra reserves of energy. He had to crawl up on his hands and knees to get there.

Reaching other mountain tops alone, Messner had felt elated and, in his words, "a witness to the whole of creation". Now, on the summit of Everest, he was too tired to feel anything. It was three o'clock in the afternoon and he had been climbing for six hours.

Messner's solo climb

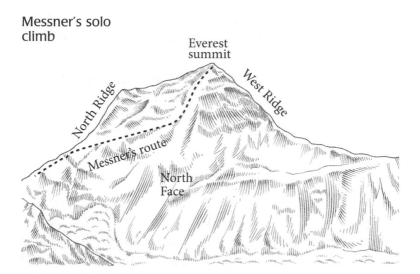

It was so cloudy, he couldn't see the usual stunning view that greets climbers who make it to the top. Looking back, he wrote: "I was in continual agony; I have never in my whole life been so tired... I am not only as heavy as a corpse, I am incapable of taking anything in."

Despite the danger of staying at the summit and getting caught in bad weather, it was almost an hour before Messner felt strong enough to return. Before he left, he managed to take a photograph of himself by attaching his camera to a special screw on his ice-axe. The journey down was easier, and it took only three and a half hours to get back to his tent. Here he was too tired to eat or drink, or even to sleep, but something in him had changed. The smell of the snow, and the different shades of the rocks, seemed more intense. He was slowly coming back to his senses. He was so tired and lying so still, he felt he could have been dead, but the thought of his success kept his spirit alive.

As he lay awake, Messner began to worry whether he had enough strength to get down the mountain alive. The high altitude was now badly irritating his lungs, and every painful cough made his stomach hurt. But luck was with him, and the dawn brought a beautiful day of bright sunshine and little wind. Leaving everything at the camp apart from his ice-axe and camera, and not even bothering to eat or drink, he edged down the mountain in a robotic trance, remembering almost nothing of the climb back to his Base Camp. But each step brought him nearer to safety. Slowly it began to dawn on him that he was going to live through his extraordinary climb.

❖

Down beneath the North Col, Nena Holguin peered up at the mountain through the telephoto lens of her camera. It was the tenth time that morning she had searched for a sign of Messner, and she was growing concerned. She left the camp site to find water to wash and, as she returned, she caught a glimpse of a tiny figure, moving high on the ridge up by the Col. The figure was moving with some hesitation, exhaustion even. It lurched here and there, as if drunk, but it could only be Messner. Nena burst into tears. At least her boyfriend was still alive. She threw on her mountaineering clothes and rushed up the slopes to meet him.

Only when Messner reached Nena Holguin did he finally allow himself to believe he had succeeded. In his exhaustion he began to hallucinate, feeling both that he was dissolving before her and that he had turned to glass. Then he began to cry. Nena led him back, and looked after him.

The next day Messner did not even have the strength to stand. It took a week before he felt he had recovered. But he had achieved what he set out to do – and his solo climb to the summit is one of the most extraordinary feats of mountaineering ever recorded.

"Not a place for humans"

The commercial expedition disasters of 1996

By the early 90s, Everest had been climbed so many times, and by so many different routes, it had begun to seem less challenging – and less alluring. In the spring of 1993, no less than 40 climbers reached the summit in a single day. On his radio show at the time, Danny Baker even joked that there were plans to build a *MacDonald's* at the top of the mountain. But in due course, Everest would strike back.

In the pre-Monsoon season in April/May 1996, there were 11 teams on Everest intending to climb to the summit via the well-known South Col route. Five of these were made up of top-grade mountaineers, but the other six were so-called "commercial expeditions". These were the ultimate outdoor adventures, where climbers paid up to $65,000 to be taken to the top of Everest by guides. The fact that such expeditions had come into existence was a clear indication of how everyday the climbing of Everest had become. Of course the climbers on these trips (referred to by their guides as "clients") were not novices. They were people with considerable mountaineering experience, and well prepared for their ascent. But they were not the same class as the world-class mountaineers who had climbed Everest in the previous decades.

Despite the obvious risks of amateur climbers trying to reach the summit of one of the world's most dangerous mountains, no one could accuse the commercial expeditions of the 1990s of short-changing their customers. Their equipment was good, they were all supplied with oxygen, and were even issued with a phial of dexamethasone for use in emergencies. This drug combats the effects of high-altitude sickness and gives a climber an energy boost. The guides on the trips all carried radios, and were men and women of great experience and courage.

Rob Hall, for example, the impressively tall expedition leader for the "Adventure Consultants" company, was a New Zealand climber in his mid-30s, who had made the summit of Everest four times prior to 1996. The company's carefully worded brochure told clients: "Skilled in the practicalities of developing dreams into reality, we work with you to reach your goal. We will not drag you up the mountain – you will have to work hard – but we guarantee to maximize the safety and success of your adventure." Hall's record was good too. In five years he had taken 39 climbers to the top of Everest.

Hall's climbers may have been amateurs, but they were deadly serious about their mountaineering. Among them on this trip were three doctors, including the successful American surgeon Beck Weathers, a Japanese woman named Yasuko Namba, and an American journalist, Jon Krakauer. He was an experienced mountaineer, and was coming along to report on commercial expeditions for the climbing magazine *Outside*. Along with Hall they would be climbing with two experienced guides, Andy Harris and Mike Groom, and a party of Sherpas.

Still, serious or not, Krakauer, with his jaundiced reporter's eye, concluded that none of the paying mountaineers in his group would have been good enough to take part in a real expedition, where climbers are chosen on merit. In fact, Krakauer thought they wouldn't stand a chance of scaling Everest without all the help and assistance Hall's company could provide.

Another commercial expedition on Everest that spring was Scott Fischer's "Mountain Madness" group. Fischer was a tall, handsome and charismatic leader. With him were two very capable guides, American Neal Beidleman and Russian Anatoli Boukreev. Boukreev was a mountaineering legend all on his own. He had been up seven 8,000m (26,000ft) peaks, all without oxygen, and had climbed Everest twice. He was tough, and as tall and strong as Scott Fischer, although perhaps not as likeable. He saw his job as ensuring his clients got to the top – after all, that was what they had paid their huge fees to do. But he was not a sympathetic, helpful man. "If client cannot climb Everest without big help from guide," he explained in his grammatically uneven English, "this client should not be on Everest. Otherwise there can be big problems up high."

Fischer's clients were a strong bunch. Among them were Charlotte Fox, an American who had already climbed two of the world's 8,000m peaks, and another notable woman mountaineer, New York socialite and journalist, Sandy Hill Pittman. Tall, glamorous and extremely rich, Pittman had already climbed the tallest mountain on six of the world's seven continents. For her, Everest was the final challenge.

❖

With so many expeditions on the mountain at one time, it was essential that an understanding be reached on when each team would go for the summit. Rob Hall and Scott Fischer knew each other well and had a good relationship, despite their commercial rivalry. They decided they would go up together on May 10. It was a fateful decision.

Their teams encountered no mishaps on the way up to the South Col. After a night in this windswept wilderness, 33 climbers, guides and Sherpas prepared to make their way up the mountain. Hall and Fischer got together and agreed that Hall's team should set off up the South East Ridge half an hour before Fischer's, because Hall's team contained less able climbers. As it was, Fischer's team soon caught up with Hall's, and the two parties mingled together on the way up the Ridge.

The night of May 9 had been a clear, bright one, promising good weather for the day ahead. But the Mountain Madness and Adventure Consultants parties had been let down by mistakes which would cause crucial delays. Any trip to the summit requires speed, as climbers must undertake the dangerous return journey back to their tents before nightfall. On the return, they are exhausted and much more likely to make silly mistakes, while their physical weakness makes them prone to frostbite and hypothermia (abnormally low body temperature).

To speed up the trip to the summit, fixed ropes were supposed to be placed along the South East Ridge but, due to a misunderstanding, this was not done all along the route. Valuable time was lost while the guides set up these ropes for their clients to climb. Then, at the South Summit, there were supposed to be supplies of fresh oxygen. These too were missing, and the two teams wasted more time waiting for Sherpas to bring up the oxygen which should already have been there.

All this added to an already alarming situation. With so many climbers going for the top, lines developed at difficult stages of the mountain, such as the Hillary Step, where ten or so climbers waited in turn, like passengers at an airport check-in desk.

As the day progressed, Jon Krakauer's suspicions about his fellow climbers were borne out. Of his party, only he, an American climber named Doug Hansen and Yasuko Namba would reach the summit.

Fischer's much stronger team had all reached the top. Here, Charlotte Fox felt no great elation – just relief that she had made it. Looking around the extraordinary 100-mile view from the summit, she recalled experiencing "a deep fear that this was not a place meant for humans".

All the climbers knew that they had a "turn around time" – a specific hour when they should turn back if they had not reached the top. But no one could remember whether it was one or two o'clock in the afternoon. Besides, everyone had made this trip to get to the summit – having spent $65,000 and being so close to achieving a lifelong ambition, many were tempted to throw caution to the wind. Then, once on the summit, some of the climbers lingered far longer than they should have done. This was not just recklessness. The combination of high altitude and exhaustion creates a strange, hallucinogenic state of mind, where the passing of time goes unnoticed.

Some climbers from both expeditions were still on top of the mountain at four o'clock. Expedition leader Rob Hall was the last to leave, together with Doug Hansen, who had failed to reach the summit on a previous attempt with Hall the year before. Hall decided he would do everything he could to ensure Hansen succeeded, but in doing so, he delayed their return journey even further.

The hold-ups earlier in the day were now having serious consequences. Getting to the top had drained Hansen of all the strength he had. When his oxygen ran out shortly after he and Hall began to come down the mountain, his life was in very serious danger.

Waiting at the South Summit was Andy Harris, one of the Adventure Consultants guides. He too was suffering from exhaustion and altitude sickness, and was feeling very confused. Hall spoke to him on his radio, and Harris managed to climb up to the summit ridge with two bottles of oxygen. But some time after meeting up with Hall and his struggling client, both Harris and Hansen fell off the mountain. Hall himself had to stop at the South Summit. He could not get the oxygen tank that Andy Harris had brought him to work, and he was too weary to carry on down.

❖

Many climbers were still high on Everest at six o'clock that evening, with darkness only an hour away. Mountain Madness leader Scott Fischer found his strength rapidly fading away. This particular climb had exhausted the normally strong and resilient mountaineer.

With problems rapidly mounting, the weather then stepped in to make things worse. Snow had fallen during the afternoon, making the route back even more slippery and tiring than it had been before. Then, in a final twist of ill luck, a deep, booming sound rolled across the top of the

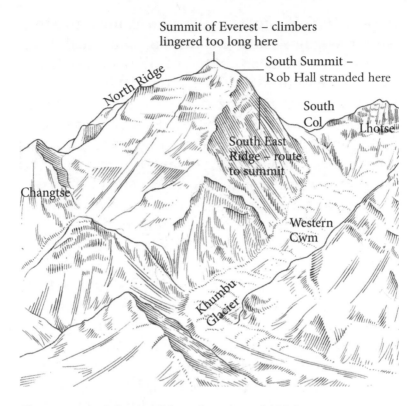

Summit of Everest – climbers lingered too long here

South Summit – Rob Hall stranded here

North Ridge

South Col

Lhotse

South East Ridge – route to summit

Changtse

Western Cwm

Khumbu Glacier

The commercial expedition disasters of 1996

mountain. Some of the climbers thought there had been an avalanche, but this was thunder. Almost immediately, the weary mountaineers were enveloped in a thick blizzard, with thunder and lightning playing around their exhausted heads.

Among the returning climbers was a group from both expeditions, including Charlotte Fox, Sandy Hill Pittman, American climber Tim Madsen, the

129

surgeon Beck Weathers and Yasuko Namba. Together with the guide Neal Beidleman, they had been wandering blindly around the Col, perilously close to the Kangshung Face. They only stopped in the blizzard when they realized they were on the edge of a deep, dark void. Now they had decided their best hope lay in trying to stay where they were, although the wind was blowing at 110kmph (70mph) and the temperature had dropped to -40°C (-40°F). This was a desperate measure, but preferable to the near certainty of falling off the mountain.

The beleaguered party did their best to ward off frostbite by slapping each other to keep their circulation going. But tired, thirsty, hungry, and out of oxygen, they were textbook cases for mountaineering casualties. As they all began to weaken in the face of the storm, they huddled together for warmth. Charlotte Fox recalled: "we just lay together in a heap and waited, I hoped, for that warm fuzzy feeling that comes with hypothermia, and death."

But as they faded away to unconsciousness, the storm blew itself out. Now it was possible to see far enough ahead to make a moonlit search for the tents. Some of the party had strength enough to get to their feet and walk towards the camp, but others were too drained of energy to move. Fortunately, the Mountain Madness guide Anatoli Boukreev had emerged from the shelter of his tent to try to find his fellow climbers. He loomed up before them, and led

Fox, then Pittman, then Madsen, back to their tents. Fox was so cold, she recalled, "I had the weird sensation of my eyes freezing inside my head".

But Namba and Weathers were not so lucky. Boukreev had rescued the climbers from his own expedition, but he did not have the strength to help Hall's clients – and anyway, he thought Hall and his guides would be out to get them. But Hall was high on the mountain, and Harris was dead. Only Mike Groom was left, and he was so frost-bitten and exhausted he couldn't even speak. When others from Hall's party found Namba and Weathers the next morning, they were so badly frost-bitten and close to death it was decided to leave them there, to let nature take its course. This might seem callous, but the decision was made with the best of motives, and with a great deal of heart-searching. There were other injured and frost-bitten climbers who had a much greater chance of survival, and it was best to concentrate on ensuring they got back down the mountain alive, rather than to waste precious time and energy on two climbers who would almost certainly die.

In an even worse predicament was Mountain Madness leader Scott Fischer. He had collapsed on a ledge 350m (1,200ft) above the Col and, like Rob Hall, had spent the night out in the open.

Boukreev didn't realize this had happened until early the next morning. Having slept for barely two hours after his climb to the Summit, he rallied the

Sherpas to make a rescue attempt. But the Sherpas who had been with Fischer the evening before said he was as good as dead. Oxygen had not revived him, and he had not even been able to swallow the hot tea they had given him. Besides, more bad weather was on the way. But Boukreev was having none of this. Scott Fischer was his friend and his employer, and if he was still breathing, he could still be rescued. He spent the day trying to persuade other climbers to help him. Finally, in desperation, he decided to go up the South East Ridge alone.

Shortly after he left the South Col camp, Boukreev saw an extraordinary sight ahead of him. Staggering through the snow was the ghostly figure of a man. He walked with great weariness and held up his hands, which were without gloves, in front of him. Boukreev thought he looked like a surrendering soldier.

As the two men edged towards each other, Boukreev realized this figure was not Scott Fischer; it was Beck Weathers. Beck was incoherent, having spent a night and most of the day left for dead out in the Col. He was rambling wildly about how he was never, never coming back to these mountains. The fact that he was alive was extraordinary, but Weathers' hands were so badly frost-bitten he would eventually lose both of them.

Rather than feeling disappointment that this staggering figure was not Fischer, Boukreev was heartened. After all, if Weathers had survived a night and a day outside, Fischer could too. He pressed on up the mountain, disappearing into the teeth of a blizzard and the fast-falling darkness. It was seven o'clock in the evening when Boukreev came across the frozen body of Scott Fischer. The zipper of his jacket was open, and one hand was without a mitten. There was no pulse and Fischer was not breathing.

Just as Boukreev was coming to terms with the fact that his friend had died, the weather grew even worse. How he got through the dark, the snow, the wind and the cold is a mystery, for he could barely see the route ahead. But Boukreev was a climber of extraordinary skill, strength and heroism. Eventually he found his way back to the South Col, and collapsed in his tent.

❖

Rob Hall had also spent a long, terrible night on the South Summit, tormented by the cold, the wind and the snow. But this tall, wiry, bearded man was immensely strong. By nine o'clock the next morning, he had managed to repair his faulty oxygen gear and was in radio contact with his base camp. But, despite the urging and encouragement of his fellow climbers at the bottom of the mountain, he could not find the strength to stand up and continue the journey down. Two Adventure Consultant Sherpas set out to rescue him. They were 200m (700ft) from the South Summit when the weather, which had remained very cold and windy, forced them back.

Many of those who die on Everest pass their final hours in unimaginable loneliness. Rob Hall spent much of that day talking to friends on the radio. In the early evening he was even able to speak to his wife – patched into his radio via a phone call from New Zealand. Perhaps this was an even more wrenching way to die – talking to a loved one, safe and warm in the family home half a world away, while he slowly had the life frozen out of him at 8,800m (28,700ft).

While they talked, she told him, "I'm looking forward to making you completely better when you come home... I just know you're going to be rescued." But she had been to the top of Everest with Hall three years before, and she knew nothing could be done to save her husband's life. They talked through a crackling, distorted line, then said their final goodbyes.

After that, there was silence. All subsequent attempts to contact Hall on the radio were unsuccessful. Twelve days later, two climbers heading for the summit found his body in an icy hollow, half-buried in the snow.

On those two days in May, five climbers from the two expeditions lost their lives on Everest. The event was widely featured in the media and caused a sensation all around the world. It did, after all, read like the plot from some disaster movie – great courage, selfless heroism, and a cast of glamorous characters dying one by one in the most dramatic location imaginable.

"The wind passeth over it, and it is gone"

The 1999 expedition to find Mallory and Irvine

George Mallory and Sandy Irvine exercise a strong grip on the imagination of the world's mountaineers. When Edmund Hillary first reached the top in 1953, he checked for any sign that the two English climbers had got there before him. Even Reinhold Messner had thought of them as he approached the summit during his epic solo climb in 1980. It was not just the bravery and tenacity of this charismatic pair that caught the imagination, for they left behind a mystery that remains unsolved to this day.

When news of their deaths broke, it was widely and sentimentally imagined they had reached the summit. Although the few climbers who knew Everest, including most of Mallory and Irvine's own colleagues, doubted that this was the case, no one could be entirely sure. Along with their missing bodies, there were two possible clues that lay undiscovered high on the mountain. Firstly, they would have left discarded oxygen bottles somewhere. If a bottle from that era was found, it would give some evidence as to how high they had climbed. Secondly, and most tantalizingly, it was known that one of the climbers had carried a camera. If they had reached the top, there would certainly be photographs.

Everest is such a gargantuan and forbidding mountain, the idea of locating bodies or objects on one of its vast, sprawling faces really is like looking for a needle in a haystack. But in 1975, a Chinese mountaineer named Wang Hongbao stumbled across a dead climber high on the North East Ridge, a short walk away from his camp. Judging by the clothes and equipment, the body was obviously from an earlier age of mountaineering. Four years later, Wang Hongbao was on a Chinese-Japanese expedition up Everest and mentioned this to a Japanese climber, Hasegawa Yoshinori, who knew the story of Mallory and Irvine. Wang gave a rough description of where he had found the body. The next day, Wang was killed in an avalanche. Yoshinori was convinced the body must be one of the missing English climbers, and carried the news back with him. The story broke to world-wide curiosity.

❖

It would take 20 years before anyone thought of following this up. In 1999, a group of American climbers, calling themselves the "Mallory and Irvine Research Expedition", set out to try to establish once and for all whether Hillary and Tenzing really were the first men to stand on top of Everest. More than anything else they hoped to find Irvine and, with a bit of luck, his camera.

The team were well in place on the North East Ridge by April 1999. In early May, the climber Conrad Anker made a startling discovery. While searching the slopes of the North Face he had already come across three other dead climbers. Then, he recalled: "Suddenly I saw a patch of white that wasn't rock and it wasn't snow." There, stretched out face down on the mountain, was a body. Most of the clothes had been blown off, and the remarkably well-preserved exposed flesh was as white as a marble statue.

Anker summoned colleagues on his radio, and was soon joined by other team mates. All of them knew at once they had found something extremely significant. They marvelled at the wool and tweed clothing, the rope made of plant threads, and the hobnail boots they could plainly see. Climber Dave Hahn remembered, "We weren't just looking at a body, we were looking at an era."

Name tags on the clothing quickly revealed that the body was that of George Mallory. The camera and its precious film were nowhere to be seen. However, it was well known that Mallory intended to place a photograph of his wife Ruth on the summit. No photograph was found on the body, leaving yet another riddle to intrigue those who believe Mallory really might have got to the top – although he could, of course, merely have forgotten to bring the photograph with him.

The climbers gathered some of Mallory's possessions, including a boot that had come off his foot, a pocket knife, a compass and his snow goggles, as well as several letters and notes that Mallory had been carrying with him. These were extremely well-preserved, and looked as if they could have been written the day before. Here, in the freezing-dry cold at 8,000m (26,000ft), time had stood still. One of the notes Mallory had carried up the mountain was an unpaid bill from *A.W. Gamages* of Holborn, London – "Motoring, Cycling, Sports and General Outfitters". Mallory had intended to settle his account when he returned. The company had closed decades ago.

❖

Before they set out, the expedition had been in touch with the surviving families of both Irvine and Mallory, to ask what they should do if they found either of their bodies. Now, in accordance with the wishes of Mallory's son, John Mallory, who was then 79 and living in South Africa, they prepared the body for burial. Anker, on John Mallory's direct instructions, took a skin sample for a DNA identification, and then they covered the body with rocks. In the bright, cold sunshine, the climbers huddled together besides Mallory's burial place, and *Psalm 103* was read aloud:

As for man, his days are as grass:
as a flower of the field, so he flourisheth.
For the wind passeth over it, and it is gone;
and the place thereof shall know it no more.

All of the men present were filled with a sense of awe and sadness. They were in the presence of a legend and, for once, the reality had lived up to the myth. Anker recalled how Mallory had "less gear than your average trekker", and how "if that had happened now, it would be like you'd get on the radio and you'd mobilize an army of Sherpas and a guide to haul their ass down. When I got there next to George Mallory, I thought, wow, if he had been here now he would have had a chance."

As to whether Mallory and Irvine had reached the top, one of the 1999 expedition speculated: "This guy obviously didn't let good sense get in the way of his determination. He might have done it. He was just enough of a wild man that he might just have had a good day that day and pulled it off."

❖

None of Mallory's colleagues were alive to hear the news that his body had been found. Edward Norton, commander of the 1924 expedition, died aged 70 in 1954. Climbing partners such as Geoffrey Bruce and Howard Somervell died in the 1970s, old men who had lived to see their children grow up, their nation survive a World War and lose an empire, and men walk on the moon – a feat even more extraordinary, and astronomically more expensive, but less costly in human life than the conquest of Everest.

In all that time Mallory and Irvine's bodies had lain frozen and undiscovered high on the mountain. Irvine is still to be found. Some people might say they, and all the others who have died, wasted their lives. But almost none of the thousands of climbers drawn to this alarmingly dangerous mountain in the eighty years since their deaths would agree...

Glossary

Avalanche A large fall of snow down a mountain.

Blizzard A severe snowstorm.

Chimney A vertical crack on a rock or ice face which is wide enough to climb up.

Col The lowest point between two peaks – often a flat plain.

Cornice An overhanging ridge of wind-blown snow.

Couloir A steep gully that cuts into the side of a mountain.

Crampons A rack of metal spikes that can be attached to climbing boots, to help a mountaineer climb on ice or snow.

Crevasse A deep crack in the ice of a glacier.

Cwm A bowl-shaped valley overlooked by steep rock faces.

Fixed ropes Ropes that have been attached to a mountain for the duration of an expedition.

Frostbite Dangerous medical condition when flesh on fingers, toes or other body parts freezes.

Glacier A slow-moving river of ice which forms high on a mountain.

High-altitude sickness Extreme illness and exhaustion, caused by lack of oxygen while high on a mountain.

Icefall A dangerous section of a glacier where ice is broken into huge blocks.

Monsoon A strong wind which brings extremely bad weather to Asia. Also used to mean the season when the wind arrives.

Overhang A section of a rockface which juts out, so that a climber has to approach it from underneath.

Ridge A narrow line of rock where two rock faces meet.

Scree Small rocks and pebbles.

Sherpa Literally, a member of a group of people who live near to Everest. Sherpas accompany most Everest expeditions as porters, guides and fellow climbers.

Sirdar A head Sherpa, who usually hires other Sherpas for an expedition.

Snowblindness Blindness, usually temporary, caused by the glare of the sun on snow.

South Col A flat plain at 7,860m (26,200ft), between Everest and Lhotse.

Summit The highest point on a mountain.

Traverse To climb sideways across a mountain face. Also sometimes used to mean climbing up and over a mountain, and coming down another side.

Further reading

Many mountaineers are brilliant writers. If you have enjoyed reading this book, you may find the following books are also worth a look:

Blessed Everest
by Brian Blessed
(Salamander, 1995)

A very readable general history and personal account, from the well-known British actor.

Everest – Mountain Without Mercy
by Broughton Coburn
(National Geographic, 1997)

Both a general introduction and a gripping account of the disasters of May 1996, complete with a fantastic selection of breathtaking photographs.

Everest – Eighty Years of Triumph and Tragedy
edited by Peter Gillman
(Little, Brown & Co., 2000)

A fascinating anthology of first-hand accounts, and many wonderful photographs.

Nothing Venture, Nothing Win
by Edmund Hillary
(Hodder & Stoughton, 1975)

An autobiography from the first man to reach the summit.

Into Thin Air
by Jon Krakauer
(Macmillan, 1997)

A rivetting first-hand account of the tragedy of 1996, by a climber who was in the middle of it all.

Everest
by Richard Platt
(Dorling Kindersley, 2000)

A lively look at the history of the mountain.

Climbing Everest
by Audrey Salkeld
(National Geographic, 2003)

A collection of Everest stories from this well-respected mountaineering historian.

Everest – The Mountaineering History
by Walt Unsworth
(The Mountaineers, 2000)

Generally acknowledged to be the most readable and authoritative account of Everest available.

Internet Links

There are thousands of websites about Everest. This page describes a couple of the best – you can access these sites via the Usborne Quicklinks Website following the instructions below. National newspaper sites are also a good source of up-to-the-minute news on Everest.

Everest News website
A fantastic site with links, day-to-day activity, history – in fact, everything you might possibly want to know about the mountain.

National Geographic – Everest website
This is a comprehensive site from the National Geographic organization.

For links to these two sites, go to the Usborne Quicklinks website at: **www.usborne.com/quicklinks** and type in the keywords "true stories everest". For safe web surfing, please follow the safety guidelines given on the Usborne Quicklinks website.